Instant

Instant Digital Audio

Douglas Spotted Eagle

San Francisco, CA

Published by CMP Books
an imprint of CMP Media LLC
600 Harrison Street, 6th Floor, San Francisco, CA 94107 USA
Tel: 415-947-6615; Fax: 415-947-6015
www.cmpbooks.com
email: books@cmp.com

Distributed in the U.S. by:
Publishers Group West
1700 Fourth Street
Berkeley, CA 94710
1-800-788-3123

Distributed in Canada by:
Jaguar Book Group
100 Armstrong Avenue
Georgetown, Ontario M6K 3E7 Canada
905-877-4483

For individual orders and for information on special discounts for quantity orders, please contact:
CMP Books Distribution Center, 6600 Silacci Way, Gilroy, CA 95020
email: cmp@rushorder.com; Web: www.cmpbooks.com

ISBN: 1-57820-276-0

Printed in the United States of America

05 06 07 08 09   5 4 3 2 1

This book is dedicated to Amanda and Josh. I miss you both.

Contents

Introduction

This book is an introduction to answers to questions often asked in the audio and audio for video world. For some, audio is elusive and frustrating, for others, merely a challenge.

Audio is arguably the most important element of any media presentation.

The human being is primarily an auditory animal. We hear many more things than our eyes can see, and we make many determinations about our attitude, position, and responses based on sound with no additional stimulus. herefore, getting audio right is very important. Audiences will tolerate poor images, but they won't tolerate bad audio. Have you ever noticed that people in the office will gather around a low-quality streaming video if it has good audio? But if the video is great and the audio is bad, no one will watch it. It's much more of a brain-drain to try to comprehend bad audio as opposed to bad video.

From December 4, 1877 when Thomas Edison first recorded the human voice to 1975 when Tom Stockham created digital audio recording at the University of Utah, we've come a long, long way. Imagine what it must have seemed like back in 1979 when the very first digital audio cross-fade was created by Thomas Britton (King's Row soundtrack album). Mr. Stockham passed away in January of 2004, but the debt I owe him for providing a paycheck for a young high school geek will remain open forever. Had I known at the time that I was in the company of the man who with Jules Bloomenthal pioneered what we've come to know as the DAW, I'd have paid more attention. I can only plead ignorance of youth.

On the video side, it all really started with George Lucas realizing the importance of sound in film, using over 40 tracks of audio for Star Wars. "Dick Tracy" was released in 1990 with the first-ever digital soundtrack. "Last Action Hero" and "Jurassic

Park" were also ground-breaking in terms of audio on film, as they brought forth what we know as SDDS and DTS.

The revolution will continue, as we start to see more high definition displays and high definition recording systems. Surround sound will become more and more common even from the desktop, and holographic sound may eventually become a common recording format.

In this book, you'll find tips and techniques, answers and hopefully inspirations to ask more questions. It is my hope that you'll find yourself intrigued by some of the techniques, tools, and concepts to the point that you'll want to investigate the subject more deeply.

"Instant Audio" isn't intended to be the last word in audio information; the intent is to provide enough information to get amateurs, prosumers, and professional videographers to a point of being able to ask better questions, understand the answers, and capture better audio. Maybe you don't fit into any of these categories, and are simply curious about audio and knowing more. That's great too. This book is written in a very accessible format for anyone wanting to know more about audio recording and audio for video.

You might also enjoy other audio-related books in the VASST "Instant" series, particularly "Instant Surround Sound" by Jeffrey Fisher. Surround sound is really the next big step in the audio world, and requires some experience and practice in order to best implement it for the best possible audio. Another valuable resource is the VASST website, where you'll find over 1000 tutorials, reviews, training files, and other information relating to audio, video, streaming, and media authoring software.

No book is written without a lot of involvement from other people, and I'd like to take a paragraph or two to thank them for their help in bringing this book to your bookshelf.

Iacobus, thank you for your tremendous, major contributions in writing this book. Without you, it would have never been completed. A great musician, but an even greater person. There isn't enough space to properly appreciate your help.

Tom Pauncz, thank you for keeping my head straight as we built illustrations and took photos over and over. Dorothy Cox, thank you for your patience with me, not just in this book but over all. I'm not the fastest pen in the west sometimes. Benjamin Nielson, thank you for putting your skills to good use here. Mannie, Linda, TJ, Jeffrey, Johnny, Victor, Mark, Mike, and everyone at VASST, thanks to each of you for helping out in more ways than I can enumerate.

Many of the descriptions found in this book are developed from classes I've been privileged to teach at NAB, DV Expo, Government Expo, NAMM, CES, and other trade events, and I'm most appreciative to the producers of those shows for pushing me to develop presentation skills that make these anecdotes possible.

Rudy Sarzo, thank you for first being my hero, then my friend. You are one of the most amazing people I know. No one inspires me as you do.

Steve at Audio Technica, Terry/Rich at Shure, Mike at Rode, Keith at Mackie/Loud, Bill and Milo at Echo, Adam and Kevin at M-Audio, thank you for all the support and the loan of many images found in this book. Of course the folks at both Sony Broadcast Electronics and Sony Media Software can't be forgotten; they've taught me so much about audio and video over the years... (Dave(s), Leigh, Brad, Andy, Michael, Gary, Caleb, Jack). Thanks, guys!

Brian Keane, one of the most Emmy®-winning-est producer/composers in the world, thank you so much for introducing me to great audio tools so many years ago. I'm so much better in the studio than I was back in the days of the old 80-8. William Aura, thank you for taking so much time to teach me about good compression techniques; I'd still be using dial-a-matic if it wasn't for you. Now it's all done in software and sounds pretty good, eh?

Tom Bee, thank you so much for giving me a second music career. The second time around was much better. I can't think of anyone I'd rather share a Grammy® with. (Tom produced the first-ever digital recording of Native American music, and went out on a limb with me, releasing the first-ever Native American flute CD).

Almost last but not least, thank you to KISS for inspiring me to become a musician, and to my music teacher for showing me that KISS might be a great band, but great music comes from a much deeper place. Gene Simmons rocks! (James Horner blows my mind)

There are so many more people who have been a part of my recording, composing, and producing career, that I can't name them all, but you know who you are.

To the members of communities like DMN, DVInfo.net, DVXUser, Videouniversity, and Sony's Vegas fora, thank you for helping me to grow and know what is sometimes elusive in the audio world. This book is for you.

Chapter 1

Hardware Setups

Your audio monitors are your window to what's happening with the sound of your project. This is a place that you shouldn't skimp. Acquiring good monitors from the start is important. A good set of audio monitors will become one of the most-used tools in your gear list, and as you become familiar with them, you'll find your mixes improving measurably over time. Spending a little more up front will always be well worth the expense versus acquiring cheap speakers with a goal of buying a better model later. "Penny-wise, pound foolish" is the proper axiom here. Of course, you can also over buy as well. Consider the level of your productions over the next couple of years, and consider the revenue from them, or their budgets. If you've got a $5000.00 production, it's probably not prudent to spend $10K on an audio monitoring system. Keep in mind you can always do your audio finish work in a rented room. Don't ever use home stereo speakers as your monitoring system unless you absolutely have no choice. Consumer stereo speakers are not made for referencing and usually have frequency curves created as part of the speaker design for a more flattering sound. The same goes for mixing through headphones. Don't do it! you'll regret it.

Surround Sound:

Do you really need it right now or not? Don't let the "cool" factor be part of the buying decision. If you know you'll be delivering your mixes in surround, then purchase a surround system, but be prepared for the cost. A surround system is typically a minimum of double the system cost, perhaps triple and even quadruple the cost of a stereo or two-channel system. If each monitor is $500.00 plus the cost of the LFE (low frequency enclosure) then you'll need to spend an additional $1500.00 for the center and two rear monitors. The center and rear monitors should match the right/left monitors for accurate listening results. Again, this isn't a place to skimp, but rather a decision of prudence. There are no surround systems worth owning for less than $500.00, and even that price point skirts the edge of usable/accurate systems. Plan on hitting a starting point of $2000.00 for an industry-standard system, with prices reaching upward of $8000.00 for a THX certified system.

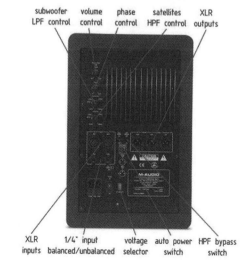

subwoofer | volume | phase | satellites | XLR
LPF control | control | control | HPF control | outputs

XLR | 1/4" input | voltage | auto power | HPF bypass
inputs | balanced/unbalanced | selector | switch | switch

Speaker size is important too. If you're in an average converted bedroom, buying a set of 12" speakers isn't a good idea, especially if you like your monitoring environment to be quiet. You'll not get the speakers working at their peak if they're not being pushed. By the same token, if they're too big, you'll not be able to push enough air in the room to hear them accurately.

Look at monitors with 6" to 8" drivers for most monitoring applications. If your room is big, consider something larger. However, a subwoofer with smaller drivers is preferential in most instances, to having large drivers and no subwoofer. The speaker enclosure will also usually have a high frequency driver. Look for a high frequency driver that is a soft dome type driver versus a Piezo-type, especially if long hours will be spent at each sitting.

A subwoofer is a separate enclosure or speaker box from the other speakers (called satellites), in the system. Its sole function is to play back bass sounds in the very low frequencies. This is where audio has the biggest challenge of being heard cleanly.

There are essentially two types of systems; one where the bass is separated out using a crossover and the same amplifier is used to power the satellites, is known as a "passive" dual bandpass. The other type uses a separate amplifier for each speaker enclosure in the system, whether it's built into each speaker or has multiple amplifiers in one box. The M-Audio LX4 system for instance, has three separate amplifiers built into the subwoofer, used to power the subwoofer and a 5 channel speaker system for surround sound use. Subwoofers are not required for mixing/recording great audio, but if you're planning on doing sound design, mixing for 5.1, or working with extended frequency sound effects such as space ships, ambiences, or other wide range audio, you'll need a sub to complete the setup.

Previously in this section, the size of the driver was mentioned. However, in terms of power ratings, there really isn't a concern for too much power. Without going deeply into the math, suffice it to say that power ratings and volume aren't relevant in the way that most editors might think. A 1000 watt

amplifier isn't louder than a 100 watt amplifier; it's merely capable of reproducing clean sound at a louder level when the audio is turned up. The more power you have, the better off you are. If you're a video editor, consider this akin to the horizontal lines of resolution of your broadcast monitor; more is better.

Generally, speaker monitors have power amplifiers built into them. This wasn't true at all in the past, but nowadays it's considered common to have a built in, amplifier that is matched to the speaker. These are called "Active" monitors. Monitors that don't have power built in and rely on a separate amplifier are "passive" monitors. There are advantages to both passive and active systems, but if cost and accuracy are prime considerations, active systems are generally preferable to passive systems. A very high quality passive system is several thousand dollars, and is becoming more and more rare with the efficient active system designs of today's industry.

Virtually all speaker monitors have some sort of crossover built into them. Having control over the crossover point is useful but not critical. The crossover is what divides various frequencies and controls which driver the sound goes to. Generally, everything below about 2.5Kilohertz is sent to the bass driver in an enclosure while everything above 2.5 Kilohertz is sent to the high frequency driver. Having a variable crossover means you can find the sweet spot, depending on the type of audio material you're working with and the type of room you're working in. Many of the lower cost monitors offer no choices, while higher end monitors like this Mackie 626 offers a number of high frequency control options.

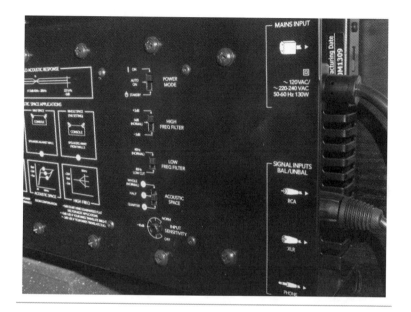

Some systems use what is called a passive crossover, others have an active crossover. The difference is that passive crossovers divide the frequencies going to individual speaker components post-amplification. Active crossovers divide the audio into frequency ranges prior to amplification. Active systems are at a minimum, bi-amplified. This means one amplifier for the low frequencies, and one amplifier for the high frequencies. A tri-amplified system has power amplifiers for the low, mid, and high frequency drivers. Bi-amplified systems are very common in self-powered speakers, and are typically very efficient. Low frequencies require substantially more power to drive the speaker than a high frequency driver, and therefore, this is a great way to optimize output. For example, the Mackie 626 illustrated here, is a bi-amplified monitor, providing 40 watts of power to the high frequency driver and 100 watts to the low frequency driver. Most of the higher quality nearfield monitors use a bi-amplified configuration. This is part of the higher cost of these generally higher quality monitors.

Be sure that the input of the monitor can support a balanced input, whether it's a TRS input or an XLR input. This is important to help prevent noise from entering the monitor chain via RF or electromagnetic interference. Further, if the monitors are to be used near a broadcast or production video monitor, be sure the speakers are magnetically shielded so that they don't create challenges with your video monitor. Most of the higher quality speakers are magnetically shielded, whereas many of the lower cost monitors are not. If you note the video monitor screen with 'bent' images, or with discoloration on one side or the other (or both), then it's quite possible that your speaker monitors are creating havoc with the image. Shielding of the audio monitor prevents this from occurring.

Low cost sound cards have almost no place in to-day's professional recording or video studio. Audio interfaces, which are often called "sound cards", are more appropriate. In choosing an audio interface, consider these points:

1. How many channels of input do you need at any given point? If you're doing voiceover work, you'll only need one channel, two at most.

2. How many channels of output do you need? If you're doing surround work, you'll need a six-channel output card. If you're doing stereo/two channel work, you'll only need a stereo/two channel output.

3. How do you want to input? XLR is always best, but maybe you'll need SPDIF (Sony Protocol Digital Interface) or perhaps you'll want 1⁄4 inch inputs.

4. How does the card connect to the computer? Firewire, USB, or PCI card are all standard I/O protocols. PCI is always the best choice, with Firewire coming in second. USB is acceptable for two channel input/output, but should never be considered for multiple channel input/output.

5. Does it need to be rack mounted? Or table top?

6. Do you want it for field work, or will it always be in the studio? If it's for field work, consider a Firewire system that can be powered from the 6-pin Firewire bus of your computer. (4 pin Firewire connections cannot pass power)

7. Price point is always a consideration, but test the audio quality of an interface that has built in pre-amps vs the quality of one that does not. Sometimes the interface with fewer features will sound better than an interface with lots of built-in features, simply because better electronics are used.

Audio interfaces have come a long, long way in recent years. While it used to be common knowledge that cheaper cards were poor and more expensive cards were the only way to go, today a couple hundred dollars goes a very long way to recording great audio. Of course, there are still very high-end cards like the Apogee Rosetta and similar models that sound great, but balancing cost versus practicality is important too. For voiceovers and monitoring, the couple of hundred dollars for an Echo or M-Audio card can go a long way. Of course if you're recording bands or particularly quiet groups with tremendous dynamics such as an orchestra, look closely at the higher-grade interfaces.

Be sure the audio interface you select has a headphone output. This will be important for not only monitoring in quiet environments, but is indispensable in tracking down audio problems and testing the audio flow at its various source points. Having an auxiliary input/output is a bonus, such as what's found in the M-Audio FW series interfaces.

Another benefit of a professional sound card is that they usually provide phantom power to condenser mics, often used in today's recording situations. Cheap computer sound cards call themselves "plug and play" power. This means they output 5 volts over the 3.5mm connector. Connecting a standard condenser microphone to this connection can damage the microphone. While there are methods of wiring the line of the condenser mics to accommodate the cheaper sound cards, you're still not achieving quality, and might as well use a card/device designed specifically for this sort of function.

Blaster-type cards are coming up in quality, and eventually we might even see professional sound cards in this format, but for the present, any card that doesn't have some sort of breakout system is likely not ready for primetime just yet. Keep in mind as well, that the interior of a computer is already a noisy place with lots of electrons flying around, and this isn't something you want to have near your microphone inputs, especially if you are using high impedance microphones, no preamp,ow-grade cabling.

Wiring

Connecting everything together is almost an art form. Planning cable runs prior to connecting everything is a good idea. Once you've measured the cable runs, add another 20% to the total length, and you should be in good shape. Cables have a way of not bending, or routing exactly as planned, or sometimes the connector sides aren't appropriately measured. Either way, plan on additional length, nearly always.

Cables come in a variety of qualities. While it's tempting to buy the cheapest or least expensive cable, it's not a good idea. Low-grade cables can allow noise to pass through if they're not properly shielded, and low cost cable connectors fail early on in the life of the cable.

Keeping all cables balanced is a good idea. What this means is that all cables are XLR or Tip/Ring/Sleeve (TRS), and the cables are wired in such a way as to keep noise minimized. High imped-ance cables can only be run for dis-tances of 15 feet or less, while there is effectively no limit to the potential length of the cable run.

Poor Connector

High quality connector

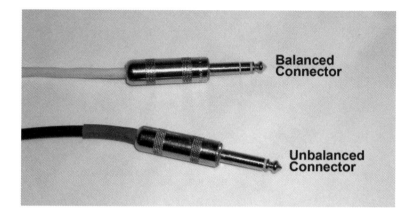

Balanced Connector

Unbalanced Connector

Low impedance cables reject noise from outside sources like fluorescent lights, radio interference, and other electronic noise sources. The way they work is by running a second cable next to the "hot" cable, with the phase inverted. This creates a noise-canceling flow of sound. High impedance cables don't have the second, out of phase cable, and therefore become "noise-at-tracters" over the length of the cable.

Depending on the number of inputs you'll have to the audio interface, you might want to consider a "snake." This allows multiple cables to be carried in one master cable, and provides for a cleaner work area. Snake cables typically come in sets of 8 channels, but they can be made to be less than 8 sets. Snake cables can terminate with a "fantail" where the connectors are just loose and are basically a collection of connectors on cables, or they may terminate in a box.

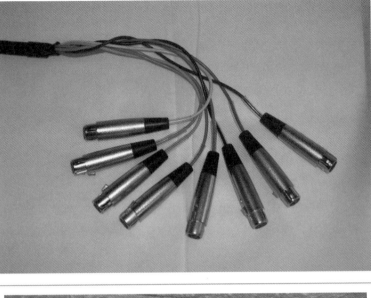

Typically, your cable runs will consist of the following:

Mic to Preamp (balanced cable)

Preamp to Audio Interface/Sound card (balanced cable)

Audio Interface to Speaker Monitors (usually balanced cable)

If you'll be using multiple mics connected to multiple preamp inputs, you'll need two cables for each channel. (one from the mic to the preamp, one from the preamp to the audio interface).

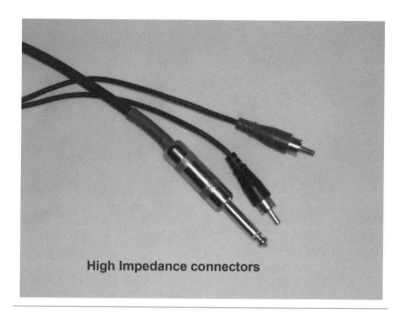

High Impedance connectors

If your microphone is a high imped-ance-only mic, be sure to keep cable runs to a minimum, and never more than 15 feet. Otherwise, you run a high risk of catching noise with the cable. Read more about this in the chapter on connecting microphones and other devices.

The high impedance connector shown in this image is often referred to as a phone connector, patch connector, guitar connector, or quarter-inch con-nector. All are different names for the same type of connection.

Mixers:

Sometimes, video and audio studios will benefit from the use of an audio mixer as an add-on to a sound card, or in some cases, in place of a sound card.

A mixer will allow for multiple microphones to be connected, processed, and output simultaneously. For example, if you are recording to a stereo mix, but need multi-channel input, you'll want a mixer. Mixers can also be used to connect CD players, VCRs, cassette decks, television audio, and virtually any other kind of audio signal for either multi-channel or dual channel output, depending on the mixer. Mixers are also known as audio desks or audio consoles. In the past, mixing consoles were huge, even for just a few channels. In recent years, mixing consoles have been reduced in footprint while growing in features.

Chapter 2

Setting up the Room for Great Audio

The room, the container of your sound, is one of the most often overlooked aspects of the recording or monitoring environment. Merely having great monitors is not nearly enough. The same can be said for microphones, preamps, and other related tools. You could easily spend tens of thousands of dollars on great gear, only to have a room destroy all the value found in that gear.

Professional recording studios dedicate a large portion of their budget to the building of a room; often more than the cost of the gear itself, because the gear can easily be changed out, but the room cannot. You don't need to do this, if you're predominantly monitoring audio, and doing the occasional voiceover.

If you're reading this book, in all likelihood your editing or recording space is a bedroom or converted office. No problem. While we can't make this sound like The Power Station recording studio, it doesn't have to sound like a bedroom.

The reason the room is so important, especially smaller rooms, is the way that the room reflects audio. Imagine a bullet ricocheting off of the walls of an all-steel room, unable to penetrate or be absorbed by the walls. Or imagine a pool ball bouncing off the sides of a pool table. However, these are not quite the same as sound. Imagine the bullet or ball being able to split different pieces off at various velocities depending on their mass. This is what audio does. It reflects differently at various frequencies.

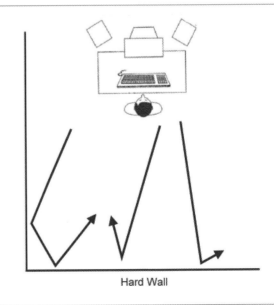

Hard Wall

In addition to this reflection phenomenon, there are other issues at play too. The predominant issue is where reflections meet themselves as a positive and negative wave. In other words, sound coming FROM the audio speaker is positive energy, while sound reflecting OFF a wall is negative energy. At one point or another, they will collide with each other. These out-of-phase energies (waves) are called "nodes". Nodes are no big deal, and are part of any room/speaker combination. It's "where" the nodes occur that are often the problem. Nodes occur from the width, height, and depth of a room..

In addition to all of this, the room will have spaces that are louder and softer at various frequencies around the room. For example, a room might be really bright and contain little bass, or a room might be muddy as it doesn't reflect the high frequencies as well, or perhaps the room simply amplifies the bass and midrange frequencies. There is virtually no such thing as a "flat" room, or a room that is balanced across the entire frequency spectrum, excluding test facilities and special designs.

Bass frequencies are the toughest to deal with. They need an entirely different treatment method than do higher frequencies. Low frequencies will mess with the overall perceived frequency response of a room, where higher frequencies are somewhat compensated for in the ear.

Monitors that are too close to the wall cause early reflections that can muddy the mix. Particularly if they are against a typical indoor studded wall on 16" centers with no insulation in the wall. If the wall is insulated, then it's helpful. If the wall is brick, even better, except that the harder wall with low absorption may present other challenges.

Maybe your editing desk has small corner shelves designed for holding CDs or DVD boxes. Often they become receptacles for audio monitors since they're not usable for much else in a video suite. Boxing your monitors into the cubby only causes the cubby and the rest of the desk to become resonant contributors to audio, creating peak points in your audio so that the resonance of the wood plays a huge part in what audio you hear.

Air/isolation is good for your speaker. If there was a way to shock mount your monitors to hang from the ceiling like you shock mount mics on a boom pole in your productions, that would be a good, if not impractical thing. The next best thing, in my opinion, is the Auralex MoPad®. These extremely dense foam stands for your speakers are worth every penny, and it doesn't take many pennies. These alone will make a tremendous difference.

Next, kill the bounce from your walls behind the speakers. Get a sheet of Sonex or Auralex Pyramids (2" or so) and put a square or half-sheet on your wall directly behind the speaker. This will help keep the sound from bouncing around inside the wall, and kill some of the reflections coming off the wall from the back of the speaker. This is particularly important if you have a speaker ported to the back like the M-Audio BX series monitors illustrated here.

Place your monitors so that your tweeters (the high frequency speaker part that sounds a little like sizzling bacon when turned really loud) are approximately at ear level. Speaker stands help a lot if you can't get them that high. Frankly, having your monitors on a different platform than your editing system is a really good thing, because then the speakers don't resonate the cabinet, as mentioned before. The speaker stands you can buy from Circuit City or Best Buy are usually just fine.

Set your speakers so the distance between the speakers is equal to the distance from the tweeters to your earlobes; in other words, a perfect triangle.

Depending on distance, it's a good idea to have something on the back wall that is absorptive. Heavy drapes, Auralex Tru-Traps®, or other absorptive and/or diffusive devices are going to help tremendously, as they absorb and deflect/diffuse frequencies that are coming back at your ears from that back wall.

The goal is to push the node points and null points as far away from the main listening position as possible. This will make a tremendous difference in what you hear. You'll still likely have some bass issues if you're in a typical editing room converted from a bedroom or office space. Usually, if you find yourself missing some bottom end/bass in a mix, consider NOT boosting the bass around 80Hz. This is the approximate frequency that most smaller rooms have a deep hole. This hole will change somewhat, depending on how far away you are from the rear wall.

Next, you've got to match the bass/subwoofer (if you have one) to the monitoring position. Don't worry too much about the balance anywhere else in the room, sometimes it's challenging to get this accomplished at just the mix position.

A great way to do this is to find a music piece that you are very familiar with, one that sounds good in the car, good in the living room, and good on the iPod. Use this as a reference point to get it sounding good in your room. I don't recommend anything that is deliberatly bass-heavy. Consider any modern symphonic movement, or a pop song mixed by a master. "Money for Nothing" from Dire Straits has been my go-to for this sort of listening and tuning experience.

Of course, if you can rent an RTA (Real-Time Analyzer) you'll be able to accurately measure the balance with its display. These are usually quite affordable, by the way.

By spending some time tuning, you'll have a substantially sweeter sounding room, and at most, it cost you less than a couple hundred bucks. A nice side effect to this process is that your ears will likely get less fatigued in long editing sessions.

All of this effort sets up the room properly for monitoring, and will help somewhat with the recording in the room. However, if this is the room that the computer occupies, you'll need to take additional steps to quiet the room enough for recording.

Before you start making these sorts of decisions, you'll need to determine whether you'll mostly be doing ADR (Automatic Dialog Replacement) or voiceover work. These two primary voice recordings are not recorded the same way.

Dialog tends to have some room ambience mixed in with the audio, but for ADR, you'll want to have a room that is fairly dead, with a small cardioid mic that can be put at a reasonable distance from the subject. ADR is less common these days, but it is still performed on a regular basis.

ADR is performed when voice tracks recorded at the scene need to be replaced, due to ambient noise from the crew, animals, traffic, or other noises. Sometimes it's not convenient to get a boom into a shot, so dialog is loosely recorded on set, and then the actor comes into the studio, watches their performance on a monitor, and re-records their lines while the dialog section loops, recording several passes. This is why ADR is sometimes referred to as "looping."

A room meant for recording ADR needs to have no real ambience to it, it merely needs to be clean, free of flutter, echo, or reverb. These audio filters and effects are all added in the post-production process. The cleaner the recording, the more that can be done with it in the post-production process.

It's a good idea to use the same mic in the field as you will be using for ADR, if you plan on only replacing a portion of the dialog. Otherwise, it will be very difficult to match up the timbre of two different microphones.

Voiceover audio is very different from ADR audio. Voiceover audio never has room ambience, and rarely has any reverb, delay, or other time-based processes applied to it. Voiceovers are intended to be very personal, intimate, and sound like the voice is in the room right next to the listener, usually speaking with authority and strength. Getting this sound doesn't require a special room at all. Even a clothes closet will work, if the clothing is still in the closet. If your voice is very loud and aggressive, you'll need a very large closet with a lot of clothing. A loud voice in a small space, without a lot of varied angles, will simply boom in a closet and likely be muddy. Low frequencies aren't affected by fabrics or soft angles nearly as much as high and mid-range frequencies are.

The most important factors in getting a good voice over are the mic, and the acoustics of the room, or rather the lack of them. We want a room that is very dry with no reflections of any kind. Refer to the chapter on microphones to learn what sorts of mics are good for voiceover work.

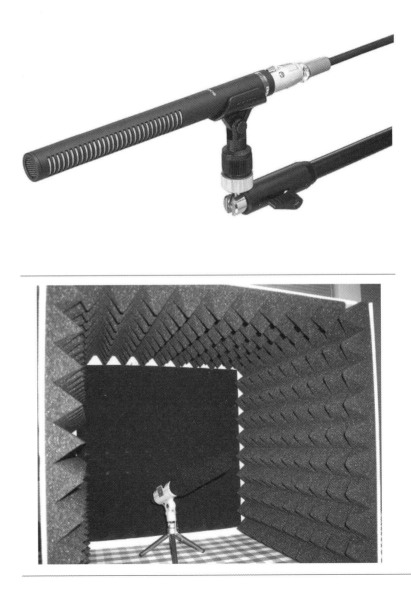

If a clothes closet isn't handy, or if you're working in a professional environment, you can build various devices to help remove the sound of the room from the microphone area. Companies like Auralex manufacture foam panels in various sizes, and these can be put together to create a great voiceover recording box. I made my first one from scrap pieces left over from a client's studio. For a cost of less than $20.00, it's cost-effective and easy to build a voiceover box like the one pictured here. To build a V/O box that can be used anywhere, follow these simple steps:

Get a 4'x4' sheet of either 1/4" plywood, or in a pinch, several large sheets of 3/8 foamcore. Cut four 24x 24" pieces of material/wood.

Obtain four 24"x24" pieces of Sonex, Acoustifoam, or similar product. Eggcrate foam used for packing will act in a similar manner if you are really on a tight budget. Keep in mind this eggcrate foam is illegal in commercial installations, and really isn't safe. It will also break down over time, but for a one-shot deal, it's acceptable.

Using spray adhesive, such as Scotch 76 spray, or other foam-safe adhesive, attach the foam to the wood or foam-core. Let dry.

Taking three pieces of the foam-covered wood/foamcore, build a three-sided box, leaving the side facing you open. Have the acoustic foam side facing the inside of the box. The adjoining edges may be simply joined with duct tape, Velcro,™ or if you are really handy, detachable hinges.

Place the fourth piece of foam covered wood/foam core on the top of the box. You should now have a box that is open only on one side, as the table top forms the bottom of the box, and the remaining 4 sides are the foam covered interior of the box.

Set the microphone inside the box, approximately halfway back, so that the front of the microphone capsule is not less than 10" from the front/opening of the box. You will find that moving the mic backwards and forwards inside the opening will allow for greater and lesser bass response. Run the cable underneath the box.

The box will eliminate air movement around the microphone, reduce/remove computer fan noise, and keep the sound entering the microphone stable and less prone to dynamic changes due to air movement. Further, you will find a more resonant, and less nasal quality to your recordings, in addition to a more "natural" sounding voice. This simple box will easily make an inexpensive mic sound like a much more expensive model, as it will lessen all outside noises and dampen a "normal" room's resonances. It will simplify your post/audio edits, and costs less than $20.00 to build.

It should also be said here, DO NOT USE THIS DEVICE TO COVER YOUR COMPUTER HOUSING!! Computer processors need airflow, cooling, and space. Covering your housing is never a good idea under any circumstances.

This box may also be disassembled and used as an absorber on a wall behind a monitor when not being used for voiceover work.

Other Room Requirements:

When setting up a room, the room's acoustics are only part of the consideration. You'll need to consider equipment layouts too, but what about the gear itself?

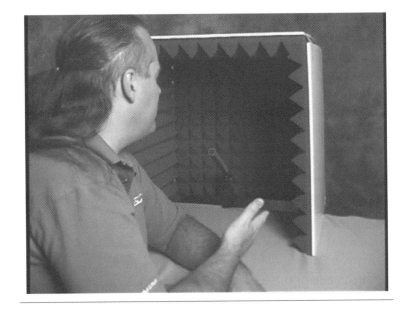

Panels mounted on foamcore can be easily tacked to any wall for absorptive/deflective needs. They can act like micro-gobos, and can be used in virtually any recording situation.

If you're recording voiceovers, you'll need a music stand, or better yet, a boom with a clamp on it. Music stands can create a reflection, unless all angles are taken into consideration. Using a boom stand with a clamp allows the reader to see the script without talking into a flat surface like a music stand. Don't forget to consider some sort of light that allows the talent to read the script without difficulty, and that can be placed so that the talent doesn't cast a shadow over the light. An inexpensive music stand light available from any home improvement store or music store will work quite well.

Consider something as simple as a seat. If you decide you want to use a typical bar stool, think again. Bar stools, unless well reinforced, will squeak when the talent shifts their weight. Stools that can rotate are potentially worse; the bearings make noise. Nervous talent will tend to swing back and forth on these sorts of seats as well.

Additionally, vinyl covered seats, or imitation leather seats tend to be somewhat noisy as well. Placing a towel over a vinyl seat will usually eliminate the squeaks that often come from these sorts of chair coverings. Be certain that all fittings and joints in your stool are tight, whether held together with screws or glue.

A comfortable desk space that is efficient yet attractive to look at isn't a necessity, but it certainly goes a long way towards improving productivity. A workspace that has the necessary tools within easy grasp is important too. The angle of computer monitors so that your body, particularly neck and back, are in alignment is very important. If your body becomes fatigued from unnatural positions, productivity and creativity are diminished quicker than you'd suspect. There are many websites on creating an ergonomic workspace; visit them and view some of the suggested options. Companies like Sausalito Craftworks/OmniRaxx build great workspaces, and if budget isn't too tight, they'll even build you a custom workstation.

Chapter 3

Microphone Types and Placement

Sound is 70% of the picture experience, and 100% of the radio or CD experience. Microphones are the first tool used in the recording process.

Microphones may be very simple, yet very complex. On the simpler side of the microphone, it's basically a speaker in reverse. If you apply voltage to a speaker, it makes sounds that you can hear. If you apply sound to a microphone, it generates voltage that the receiving device can hear. Speakers are often used as microphones, even today. One great method of recording big bass sounds is to take a large speaker and wire it with microphone connections, place it in front of a big bass rig or kick drum, and use it in combination with other mics or direct boxes to record the bass or kick drum.

There are several considerations when choosing a microphone for your recording needs. One consideration is the ability of the microphone to accurately reproduce the original sound as it is converted from audio waves to voltage.

Most microphones today are reasonably faithful once you pass a median price point, and it becomes a matter of "personality." Each mic manufacturer has their own "personality" that some users will like, and others won't necessarily appreciate.

Another consideration is "speech intelligibility." This is the term used to describe how comprehensible voices are in a recording. In the 1K to 3.5K frequency range, human hearing is particularly perceptive (or not, depending on age) and this is one place that various microphones have varied sensitivities. Many of the microphones recommended in this section have slight boosts in this range for greater intelligibility. Of course, EQ and other techniques may be employed to boost these frequencies as well, but we like to have the mic capture the sound with the boost so that we're not adding anything to the signal later in the process.

As you might guess, there are several types of mics available, and of course their price ranges reflect this as well, with mic costs starting in the sub $100.00 range going up into the several thousand dollar price points.

There are three basic mic types, and in those three types, there are several designs that utilize aspects of each of these mic types.

Microphone Types

Dynamic mics - Mics that generate their own power. These mics are found everywhere, in every situation, from rock stages to cheap computer microphones. Some types of dynamic mics have been around for years.

Ribbon Mic - Use a very thin strip of metal between two magnets. As sound waves strike the ribbon/thin metal strip, induction causes the sound waves to be converted to electrical energy.

Condenser mics - One of two plates is charged with a current. As the distance between the plates increases/decreases due to sound waves striking them, the energy is changed, thus creating the current required to reproduce sound. There are a variety of condenser microphones, such as the piezo-electric and the electret condenser.

For the moment, we'll focus on average mic designs that fall from the above three categories, as they apply to most uses in video and general audio.

Shotgun mics - Named for their appearance, not for their characteristics.

Lavaliere mics - The type that is often hidden, used by interviewers the world over, and used on most television news broadcasts.

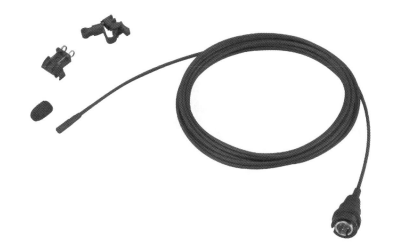

Stick mics - Mics that go on a stand, such as seen on most music stages and in the hands of field journalists.

Boundary mics - Mics that are placed on an object and in many cases, use the sound characteristics of that object to "help" the mic hear audio better.

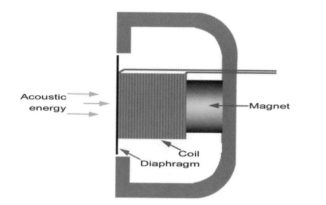

Acoustic energy → → →

Magnet

Coil

Diaphragm

The Shure SM 58 is a common dynamic mic. Far from fragile, the running joke in the rock music industry is that you can drive nails with one. Dynamics are by far the most common and familiar type of mic. The dynamic mic works by having a plate coupled to a coil (known as a diaphragm) move over a magnet when pressed upon by air pressure, creating voltage. This voltage is passed from the mic to a preamplifier, usually found in a mixer or camcorder, and amplified to a level where the voltage is sufficient for a mixer or camcorder to process and record or reproduce. In fact, if you view a cross section of a speaker, and the cross section of a dynamic microphone, they look quite similar.

Some mics have a magnet made of neodymium. This allows the magnet to be smaller, lighter, and have greater frequency response and higher output.

Dynamic mics are available in an extremely wide variety of types, brands, and price points. This mic type is very good for high SPL (sound pressure level) and general-purpose use.

Condenser mics use an outside power system, sometimes built into the mic in the form of a battery compartment, while others use an external source. The external source may be a camcorder, mixer, or powered box that sends voltage down the line. This is known as "phantom power."

Condenser is another word for "capacitor" as this type of microphone uses a capacitor to convert acoustic energy into electrical energy.

The condenser mic has two plates as opposed to the single plate of a dynamic. One of the two plates is charged with voltage. Depending on the mic, it could be the front or back plate. When sound waves strike the front plate, it moves against the distance between the two plates, generating voltage.

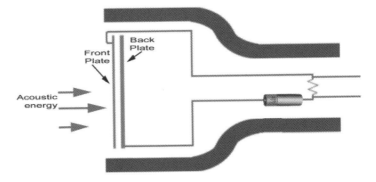

The external voltage allows the plates to be very sensitive, and typically capable of outputting higher voltage from the mic, reducing the need for a high amount of preamplifier gain, cutting down on the noise generated by the preamplifier, and typically providing a cleaner, more accurate sound.

The device illustrated provides phantom power to condenser mics that don't use batteries and there is no mixer available or necessary on the shoot.

Electret condenser mics are similar to a condenser, but don't require external power; the power required is built into the mic in the form of a capacitor, acting somewhat like a permanent magnet. Therefore, no batteries or phantom power are needed.

As a general rule, condenser mics are not optimal for high sound pressure levels, as the extreme sensitivity of the mic can make it susceptible to distortion in extremely loud circumstances. One other drawback to condenser mics is that their sound quality is affected by weather/humidity. Keep them dry, and in their cases. Usually, condenser mics come with a small packet of desiccant, or material that will absorb moisture. Keep it with the mic so it doesn't rust. If the mic does get wet, carefully shake all the water out, and put near a heat source to dry it.

These mic designs may be broken down into yet more categories: the following pages describe the pickup or "listening patterns" of various types of microphones.

Pickup Patterns: This is a description of how the mic "hears" sound, based on the direction it's facing.

Omni-Directional Mic Pattern

Omni-directional mics have a pattern just as their name implies; Omni (all) directional. These are rarely used in settings where the audio input to the mic will also be reproduced simultaneously through loudspeakers. In other words, you won't find omni-directional mics on your favorite band's stage during a live performance. There are two reasons for this. First, because omni's pick up or hear everything in all directions, the sound coming from the speakers may also be picked up and cause feedback. Feedback is where the mic hears the speakers and in turn feeds more sound to the speakers and on and on it goes. Secondly, bleed from other instruments on a stage make it difficult to control what the mic hears, so if you have a person being interviewed on a rock stage, whether they are in front of or behind the drummer, it won't matter because the mic hears the drummer regardless of what is done. The pickup pattern of an omni- directional mic is drawn as rounded when viewed on paper. (See previous illustration) Omni's are good for interviews in a quiet stage setting, good for broadcast use, and good for recording studios where the setting is controlled and reflections from walls, ceilings, floors, and instruments is a consideration for capturing the optimum sound. Omni directional microphones may be used for stereo micing a source, as they have no proximity effect.

Bi-directional (Sometimes called a "Figure of 8 mic")

Bi-directional mics, like their name implies, can pick up sound from two directions, typically from the front and rear of the microphone. Bi-directional mics reject sound from the sides. These are not to be confused with stereo microphones. Bi-directional mics are often used for interviews between two people. Bi-directionals are also good for recording two vocalists in a recording studio where the performance might be compromised if the singers were in different rooms or too far apart.

Hypercardioid Shotgun (sometimes incorrectly referred to as a "zoom" mic)

Use microphones that are made of brass, bronze, or aluminum, never plastic.

Plastic can resonate, causing the sound to be hollow and muddy.

The shotgun mic has a fairly tight pattern that rejects sound from the side, and to some degree from the rear of the microphone. Shotguns are commonly used on boom poles and in some indoor situations. Although many magazine ads depict the shotgun mic mounted on a camera, this should nearly always be a last resort. Shotgun microphones rarely work well indoors if there is any distance between the source and the mic. Shotguns are wonderful for voice-overs, outdoor recording, and may be selectively used for indoor recording.

Uni-directional

Uni-directional mics are known by many different names, and offer a variety of pickup patterns. Hypercardioid, Super cardioid, are both names for the tighter patterns of the Uni-directional mic. Unidirectionals are sometimes called "cardioid" mics because of their heart-shaped pickup patterns. They're also occasionally called "directional" mics as they are not multi-directional like an omni-directional mic is.

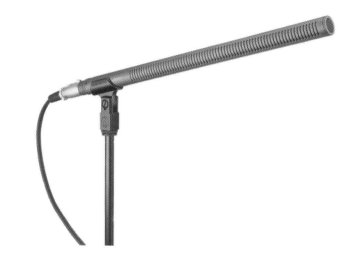

Shotgun mics come in a wide number of makes, models, patterns, and price ranges. These are the mics seen on the end of long booms, generally 8-16 inches in length, often covered by fur windscreens sometimes referred to as "dead cats" or large acoustically transparent housings known as a "blimp." Shotguns are great and usually necessary in video shoots where a stick or lavaliere microphone would be intrusive to the shot. Watch Jay Leno, Saturday Night Live, or David Letterman long enough, at some point you'll likely see the shotgun mike mounted on a boom drift into the picture at least once.

Shotguns are also exceptionally good for voice over (V/O) work and many V/O pros use shotgun mics in their work. Shotgun mics generally have a fairly narrow field in which they'll pick up audio. The further away from the source the mic is, the less audio will be picked up with clarity. However, shotgun mics are electronically and physically tuned to work a narrow 'corridor' to pick up audio from the source. This 'corridor' is known as a pattern, which is often variable in a microphone depending on the circumstances in which it's used.

Uni-Directional mic pattern

Uni-directional mics are probably the most common form of microphone. The example of the Shure SM58 is a good example of a uni or 'one' directional mic. These mics have a pickup pattern that is somewhat heart-shaped, leading many engineers to call them "cardioid" mics. The tighter the pattern is, the less sound is picked up from areas away from the mic element, or part of the mic that hears sound.

Extremely tight mic patterns are known as Hyper-Cardioid or Super-Cardioid mics These mics are extremely useful in most stage settings where a singer needs to have maximum mic sensitivity and yet have maximum rejection of farther away audio to minimize bleed into the house sound system, as well as to minimize the concern for feedback in the PA system.

Typically, these are stick mics, but by no means are all uni-directional mics stick mics.

Uni-directional mics can also be lava-lieres, shotguns, or stand-mounted specialty mics such as the boundary mic in the image shown here. These mics can be hidden, hand-held, or used as a table mic. Keep in mind that the proximity effect comes into play with all directional microphones. The proximity effect causes an artificial boost of low frequencies. Some mics have switches to help manage how the low frequencies are presented on output. Proximity effect can be used to create a very intimate, close in sound, but can also create muddiness in the sound if not used correctly. Radio DJs often "play" the mic like an instrument when it's appropriate to the dialog.

Shotguns may be mounted on a cam-corder for the 'run-and-gun' videog-rapher, but it is better utilized on its own stand, or better yet, on a boom managed by an experienced boom operator. Your next-door neighbor is probably not the best choice for a boom operator unless you can teach them what they should be listening for.

If your master camcorder is mounted on a tripod, the shotgun may sit on the camcorder if no other option is available. However, sometimes it's easier to carry a mic stand that can sit next to the camcorder, so that any camera movement does not interfere with the directional audio of the shotgun. If the shotgun is on a roving camcorder, be aware that a fast pan with the camcorder across a far reaching shot will play havoc with listeners ears, particularly if there is information that requires viewers attention. As an example, if you have someone on camera describing the beautiful cement floor they just poured, and the mic is pointing at them describing it, don't pan the camcorder across the floor as they describe the process, or the mic is no longer pointed at the audio source that the viewer should be hearing.

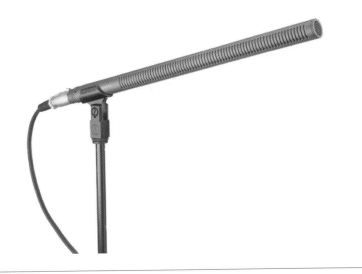

In searching for a shotgun, look for mics that are metal bodied. Avoid plastic mics like the plague. Plastic usually resonates at higher frequencies than metal, breaks more easily than metal, and plastic mics generally produce poor sound. Look for a mic that has a fairly tight pattern for most video uses. Look for a mic that has not only a solid housing, but a good mount. Make sure the mic comes with a decent foam windscreen that covers the entire length of the mic except for where the mic clip or mount might be. Windscreens can actually generate noise, if they're touching anything; keep them clear of obstruction.

Some shotgun mics have a narrow pattern, others may be switched to be a wide field mic, and yet others may be switched from mono to stereo.

The pattern is a characteristic of the mic's build. The long, narrow physical housing of a shotgun mic allows frequency filtering and phasing to be used to narrow the mic's pattern.

The mic is pointed at a source, and audio is picked up while sounds not relevant to the source are rejected. This doesn't mean that a shotgun mic may be taken into an exceptionally noisy environment and used to record a whispering interview and that the mic will reject the noise. It will give priority to the source it's pointed at, but the mic cannot reject out of hand, sounds that are coming from its sides (ambient sound). It merely hears the sounds with lesser volume than the signal it's pointed towards. Many require phantom power, or power from a device such as a battery or output from a camcorder or mixing device that provides voltage to the microphone. Shotguns actually become omni-directional in lower frequencies, and this can be problematic in highly reflective indoor areas. Be sure you know how the mic will respond when used indoors or highly reflective outdoor locations. Personal preferences for shotgun mics run towards the Audio Technica AT815ST for long-range use and the AT897 for short-range use. Sennheiser, Shoeps, and EV all make good shotgun mics as well, but they are quite pricey.

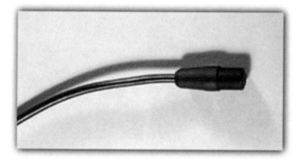

Lavaliere mics

Lavalieres, or "lavs" as most pro's call them, may be either condenser or dynamic, and may be either omni-directional or uni-directional. The Audio Technica AT 831 is an excellent example of the unidirectional mic, and is used in most of our video and live recording work. Often times, lavs will have a fairly long cable from the mic to a body/belt pack that holds transformers and electronics for the mic, as well as the battery housing.

The Audio Technica 899 subminiature lavaliere is smaller than a pencil eraser, and is available in flesh tones to be easily hidden on a video shoot. Small, adaptive, and usable in nearly any situation, a good set of lavs are practically indispensable for the videographer. In this image, you cannot see the lav mics that are placed inside the Cartier-like pens in the singer's breast pocket. Sub-mini lavaliere mics are easy to hide from the camera's view. You can hide lavs in a number of creative places such as flowers, books, or even in hair if necessary.

Lavs come in a variety of colors as well. Black or crème are the most common colors, and windscreens may be purchased for these at most pro audio shops in a variety of colors. Lav placement is always a point of contention. A good rule of thumb is to place the fist with extended thumb beneath the chin of the person to be mic'd and wherever the bottom of the fist lies, is where the lav should go. This is not a hard-fast rule of the business, but one that is comfortable and usually fail-safe. These tiny mics may also be hidden in a groom's boutonnière, in a bouquet of flowers, or even in the hollowed out top of a pen in a corporate executive's pocket.

Once, I was called on to record a group of opera singers. The singers could not have any microphones visible on stage, as that would go against the rules of opera. So, we ended up placing a lavaliere mic inside of the bodies of executive-type pens, with the insides of the pens removed. Small holes for the cable to body pack were punched in the suit pocket of each singer, and the live video shoot went flawlessly with the audience being none the wiser that the singers each had a microphone in their pocket! Lav's also are very common with wireless body packs, allowing the interviewee or other talent to move about as much as necessary. Lavs are getting smaller and smaller all the time, as illustrated in this image of the Audio Technica AT898 microphone.

Handheld/Stick mics

Stick mics are the type of mic typically seen in the hands of field journalists, often with a station ID cage/flag on the lower portion of the mic. Great for situations where a mic being in the shot isn't an issue, these are life savers, and often the least expensive of good alternatives. Stick mics are typically dynamic mics, yet there are several condenser stick mics available too. Stick mics look great in the hands of an interviewer in a field situation where passersby are being stopped and placing a lav is simply out of the question due to time, opportunity, or simplicity. Stick mics are also nearly the only type of mic found on a rock stage, with exceptions being made for performers that use headset mics.

Stick mics can be used for recording voiceovers and picking up audio in close quarters or loud environments. However, stick mics aren't very useful for general audio purposes, as they are typically designed for close in work. Use stick mics for recording vocals, close to an instrument, or close to a sound source. Remember, directional stick mics will have the proximity effect; be sure you know how to manage this so that you can prevent muddy audio.

Boundary mics

Boundary mics are often part of a
permanent installation, and are rarely
part of the production videographer's
bag of tricks. However, these oft-over-
looked mics are terrific for videographers, particularly event or wedding
videographers. Boundary mics are
usually affixed to a surface, where the
surface becomes a part of the sound-
generating field. Sometimes podiums
or choir lofts contain boundary mics,
as do many courthouses, etc. However, they are excellent for recording
the sound of tap shoes, dancers feet,
or working in rooms with medium to
extreme ambience and the room sound
is the desired sound. Boundary mics
are not great for ambient room recording, but they generally have excellent
rear-rejection characteristics that
make them quite powerful in noisy
rooms where there is an audience and
a focused point sound source. They
can easily be concealed in a variety of
locations, and some can be painted to
match décor.

There are several types of boundary mics, some working on pressure, such as the PZM or Pressure Zone Microphone, and others that are standard dynamic or condenser style mics. These mics are strategically engineered so that the mic element is positioned to pick up sound from a surface, rather than a direct pick up of sound. Often times, choirs and large orchestras are mic'd for television broadcast by using boundary mics mounted to a sheet of clear Plexiglas, allowing the camcorder or audience to see through the transparent plastic, or have a mic in a space where anything not transparent would mar the appearance of the room. Boundary mics are often used in dance productions where the sound of feet or shoes must be heard, or where body mics aren't a possibility. These mics have limited use in a live environment, but are often very valuable in a recording or video environment. The AT 811RX Boundary microphone is great for recording large groups around a table, micing a wide stage area.

There are also other mic types, such as Piezo Electric mics, but these are typically found in in low-grade audio situations such as telephones and computer mics. Piezo electric mics have very limited frequency response, and so are generally used for very specific applications in the professional recording world, such as bridge-mounted acoustic guitar pickups and harmonica mics like the old CAD HM50 mic.

In a recording studio, large diaphragm mics are commonly found for micing vocals, large drums, and other large, high volume instruments. Small diaphragm mics are often used with acoustic guitars, smaller instruments, and high frequency percussive instruments. Most sound engineers and producers have their own favorite microphones, with their opinions based on years of experience with various tools. As you keep working with audio, you'll likely develop your own preferences. In the mean time, one can only do research to determine what mics will best suit your purposes. However, don't get caught up in too many opinions without trying to form your own from experience.

One school I recently taught at had a group of students that had read an article or review about the AKG 414. One of the teachers really liked the mic too. So, when the time came to mic the singer and I didn't use the 414, one of the students lost a little respect for me. Rather than argue with him, I simply replaced the Shure SM91 with the 414, and handed him the headphones, and asked the singer to sing the song again. He was a little sheepish as he realized that this equipment is merely a tool, and getting hung up on a specific tool is a quick way of limiting options. Ironically, the school had a fantastic selection of ProTools hardware and software, and every conceivable mic, preamp, and other outboard gear an engineer could dream of. But several students were hung up on some ideas they'd read about instead of actually working with the gear they had.

The Ribbon mic

Ribbon mics are rarely used in the world of audio-for-video, may be used on occasion. Ribbon mics are generally quite fragile, and low in output. However, they offer a stunning detail/frequency response due to the very thin metal used in the ribbon. Ribbon mics can easily be destroyed by excessive SPL striking the ribbon. Modern ribbon mics such as the Royer 121 can manage fairly extreme SPL, but it's also a very pricey microphone at a cost of US$1200.00. However, even with the newer materials found in these ribbon mics, preventing pressured air from hitting the ribbon is desirable. We mic kick drums at a distance of about 6 feet, so as to prevent the ribbon from being hit with too much energy and breaking. Ribbons can also fatigue over time, due to the constant flexing of the thin metal.

Reading Frequency Response Charts

All microphones with any reputation, include a frequency response chart. You can usually find these in catalogs, or on websites. These tell you how the microphone is going to reproduce sound-waves, or how it "hears" the sound.

While some folks would like to have all microphones read flat across the spectrum, most mics can't do this, and what sets one microphone apart from another is "personality." Each mic has its own personality, and just like people, mics aren't always sociable with other mics or with certain instruments. Even if a mic were perfectly flat, it likely would demonstrate some deviation depending on temperature, humidity, and fluctuating voltage as in the case of a condenser mic.

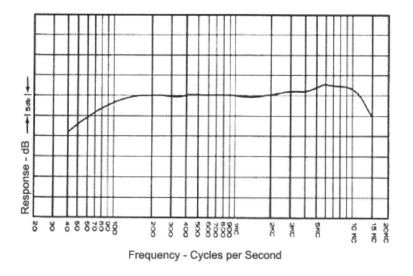

Response - dB | 5 dB

Frequency - Cycles per Second

The Horizontal axis in this image, defines the frequency in Hertz, and the vertical axis indicates decibels. A line going higher than the center point indicates that there will be exaggerated frequencies at that particular point, and a line dipping below center point indicates decreased levels of that particular frequency point.

Generally, you'll want mics tailored to your purposes. For example, a mic designed for smooth response to a kick/bass drum likely won't be useful for most dialog purposes, unless you're looking for a deep, resonant sound with a potential to be muddy or boomy. To the converse, a Shure SM 58, designed for live stage vocals, doesn't sound terrific as a violin mic.

In the world of audio-for-video, you'll want to have at least one lavaliere and a hypercardioid microphone. The lav can be used for body placement or hiding near a sound source while the hypercardioid can be used as an on-camera mic when absolutely necessary, but can be used on a boom, on a stand, near a sound source, and for voiceovers. A shotgun microphone is great, but has limited uses. We'll cover that later in this segment.

Microphones always work best when they're close to their sound source. For interview work, a lav is virtually always the first choice when you have control over the recording situation. The lav needs to be properly placed, just over the thickest part of the sternum where the clavicles meet the breastplate. This is where the bone is the thickest, and has the least resonance. Of course, the lav can go other places, such as under a collar, in the hair, or hidden in a handkerchief or boutonnière. Wired or wireless, this is often a first choice.

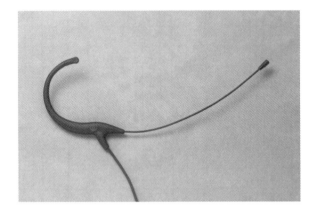

My personal favorites (in no particular order) depending on budget:

- Audio Technica 831b

- Audio Technica 899

- Audio Technica 892

- Sony ECM 55

- Sony ECM 66

- Countryman B3

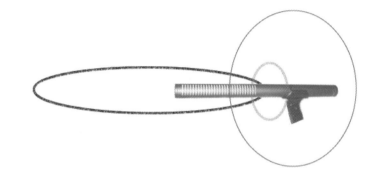

The hypercardioid is a great mic type for use in a variety of situations. Depending on where you're capturing audio from, it might be the best choice, always. For use on a boom, marketing might suggest that you must use a shotgun microphone. If you're working outdoors in a wide-open area, this is likely true. However, shotgun microphones rarely work well indoors. Depending on the design of the shotgun and the type of the room being recorded in, the shotgun microphone will actually sound worse indoors than it will sound outdoors.

Shotgun microphones tend to be omndirectional in the lower frequencies, and more importantly, if the shotgun hears reflections from the room at the same volume or level as the originating sound, the shotgun will be very confused as to what sound it should accept and what it should reject. The reflections will color the sound. This is why a hypercardioid such as the AT 4053 are great; they sound good in a room, while rejecting much of the room's sound. They also have a high degree of speech intelligibility. One of the standards in the industry is the Schoeps CMC641, but there are several lower-cost alternatives such as the Rode' NT3 mic or the Audio Technica 4053.

There is a rule in the audio world of what is known as 4 to 1. While this mostly applies in the live sound realm, it is somewhat applicable to the video world if you're mixing audio from a live stage or multiple microphones.

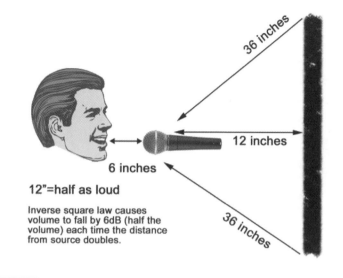

36 inches

12 inches

6 inches

12"=half as loud

Inverse square law causes
volume to fall by 6dB (half the
volume) each time the distance
from source doubles.

36 inches

Put simply, you take the maximum distance from the microphone to its sound source, and multiply it by a factor of 4. This is the distance that microphones should be away from each other. So, if you have a microphone that is 2 inches away from the sound source, then the next closest mic shouldn't be closer than 8 inches. However, this isn't always possible, so be aware of the rule as you place the on-axis point of a microphone when it will be near another mic receiving similar sound sources. Not being aware of this rule could potentially create odd phasing or comb filtering as sound bleeds from one source microphone to another, when these sounds are mixed together. In situations where you have little choice, consider using boundary type mics, as they are less susceptible to problems from close placement.

Microphone Placement

Microphone placement is everything. As stated earlier, a cheap mic close to the sound source is better than an expensive mic placed far away; different microphone types have different optimal placement positions.

Shotgun Microphones

Shotgun microphones are a great choice for recording a subject whether from a distance while rejecting any ambient sounds around the subject or up close. You'll see shotgun mics typically mounted on boompoles for the boom operator to move around and control. For more information on using boompoles, refer to Chapter 7, "Effective Mic Boom Techniques."

When using stereo shotgun mics, pay attention to the marking (typically marked as, "up") on the mic so that you know that that is where the mic's top is in order to be sure the correct stereo field is being recorded.

When mounting a shotgun mic onto a camera, there are several things to keep in mind. Always use a shock-mount so that no bumps on the camera get transferred to the shotgun mic. Don't use a shotgun mic that is too long for multiple reasons: The shotgun may enter the camera's field of view, which you obviously do not want, and the Uni-directional shotgun mic may be too lopsided and heavy. Similarly, the shoe mounts on most DV cameras are not typically designed for the longer, heavier shotgun mics. You may damage the camera's mic mount if the mic is too lengthy.

Also, do not try to balance longer shotgun mics by bringing them back farther into the mount; shotgun mics were designed to be held in only one location, which is towards the back.

Stick (or Handheld) Mics

Stick mics were originally designed for a live situation on concert stages due to their tight pickup patterns and rejection outside the pattern.

Stick mics usually come in two flavors: Hypercardioid or cardioid. A hyper-cardioid mic has a very tight pickup pattern. A cardioid mic has a larger pickup pattern. Stick mics are usually best as close to the mouth (but not on the mouth) as possible. Stick mics can be placed on the chin or under the nose for a full sound.

Lavaliere Microphones

Lavalieres should be placed as close to the sternum as possible. You can easily achieve this by "hitchhiking." Simply stick your thumb up as if you were hitchhiking and then place your thumb against your lower lip. Where you fist ends up is the optimal position where the lavaliere mic should be.

Note that this lav placement is not the case in every situation. Sometimes you see them placed around the subject's midsection or even lower on TV; keep in mind that this is a very controlled environment. You may even see lava-lier mics placed somewhere around the subject's collar; this is just fine if you don't have any other choice. As a general rule, though, you want

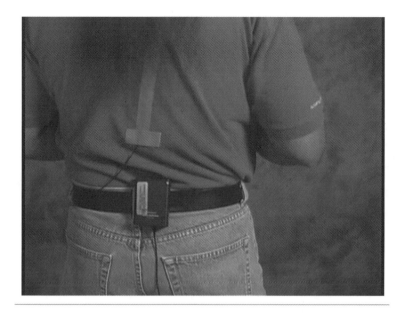

lavaliere mics to be as close as to the sternum area as possible.

Also, sometimes it is crucial the mic be hidden, such as in an operatic performance. You may have no other choice but to place the mic so that even though it is not in the optimal postion, it's hidden from view.

There are few choices available for mounting a lavaliere mic. Besides the typical clip mount, some lav mics also have buttonhole mounts. Some even have magnetic mounts that allow very flexible placement on the subject's body. One of the great things about lav mics is that they can virtually placed anywhere

Body packs for wired mics should be placed in the small of the back. Gaffer's tape should be used to guide the mic's cable up the subject's back.

Don't use duct tape; it will leave residue on a subject's clothing. Use gaffer's tape instead.

When recording indoors, you may not want to use a windscreen on a lavaliere mic, as this may cause noise as the mic moves/scrapes against a subject's clothing. In the event that you must use a windscreen, wrap a small piece of silk over the windscreen and secure it, which should eliminate any scraping noise.

You don't have to go out and buy a pre-made pop-stopper. You can make your own by stretching nylon stocking over a coat hanger. However, it may be a little tough to secure the homemade pop-stopper to the mic stand. Pre-made pop-stoppers usually come with a clamp that easily adjusts to clamp onto a mic stand.

> Use real silk, not synthetic polyester silk.

Large Diaphragm Microphones

Large diaphragm mics are the mic of choice for voiceover and studio work. You may also see large diaphragm mics used on boompoles as well.

Instead of a pop-stopper, you can also tape a pencil or pen right in front of the center of the diaphragm. This will also break up the harsh sibilants in your voice.

Large diaphragm mics are always placed in a shockmount due to their sensitivity. These types of mics are also very sensitive to air pressure, so any hard sibilants like hard P's (such as in "papa" or "pop") are going to be harsh. That's where a pop-stopper comes in. Pop-stoppers diffuse the hard sibilants so that they don't harshly affect the sensitive diaphragm in a large diaphragm mic.

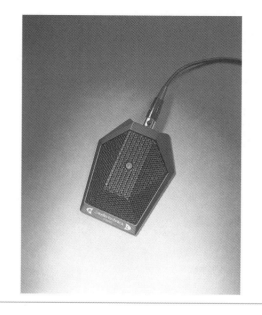

Boundary Microphones

Boundary microphones are designed for a group situation such as in a courtroom or in a corporate boardroom. They can also be used in a situation such as a play by placing the boundary mic on the stage.

Boundary mics are also known as hemicardioid mics. These types of mics have a large pickup pattern that picks up equally well from the front and sides. They have excellent rejection from the rear.

Boundary mics change their pickup behavior based upon the surface they're resting on. They work best on a hard surface due to using the hard surface as a conductor for its resonance. The larger the boundary mic, the more robust they sound.

Stereo Microphones

Stereo microphones are a great choice when you want to record a source in stereo, like a crowd at a concert or the ambient sounds of a swamp. Another great thing is the stereo field of the mic is more pronounced the farther the sound source is away from the mic.

Make sure, as always, that the stereo mic is oriented the right way so that the stereo field is set up correctly. Look for the on/off switch on the mic and make sure it's facing up. This will tell you the mic is oriented correctly.

Placement is critical

You need to find the sweet spot in a microphone in order to obtain an optimal recording.

> **The proximity effect is the increase in the bass response of certain mics as the distance between it and its sound source is decreased.**

There is more to great audio that simply connecting a microphone to a recording device and getting started. Getting the mic in the right place takes time, a gentle ear, and practice. Eventually, knowledge of various places to start becomes part of the professional's arsenal. However, never will you be able to simply walk into a recording situation and throw down a mic and immediately start recording without first checking placement through some sort of a monitoring system.

Here are some techniques and tactics to start with when it comes to placing mics.

Close Micing: Get the microphone within approximately six inches to the sound source. With dialog, this is easy in most situations, getting the microphone on a lapel or shirt front, or in the case of voiceovers, on a stand. Close mics will offer a more intimate sound, sometimes very breathy and personal. Higher quality mics will sound great this close, while even cheaper mics will sound pretty good.

For a different effect/quality of sound on a voiceover, try raising the mic just above eye level so that the voice/mouth is lifted up towards the mic. This causes the throat to open and offer the nasal passage a better flow of air, and will change the voice somewhat. Depending on the voice, this can easily help provide a richer and clearer voice recording. I once saw a voice-over artist use a heavy exercise rubber band on her jaw, so that when she spoke, she had to fight the elastic band. She claimed that fighting the band gave her better diction. She has a great voice, so I can't comment much on her unorthodox technique.

Good Technique

Less efficient technique

As you start to experiment with mic placement, you'll quickly notice that the timbre, or tone of the voice or other source being recorded. This is part of the practice, learning how to quickly identify the location that creates the sonic presence you're looking to achieve.

Audio waves will reflect from virtually any surface which is why distance and absorption material help to eliminate ambient reflections.

Our ears hear differently based on sight. What this means is, visual cues will help us understand what we're hearing. Further, our ears and brain are hardwired to ignore or filter sound in live situations. Perhaps you've been shooting in a large auditorium, and the sound while you were there was great. But when you got back to the studio or editing room, the audio was muffled, grainy, and distant. This is because the microphone hears sound as it really is where your ears most likely were filtering all the reflections in the live environment. (This is also why it's critical to wear headphones to monitor sound as it's being recorded)

Distant Micing: Anything past about 24" falls into this category. Distant micing can be a challenge, depending on the mic, the room, and other circumstances. Sometimes it can be a huge help in getting the right sound, but this falls into the "listening" category.

Place the mic approximate to the sound source, usually pointing directly at the sound source. Put headphones on so you can monitor the sound directly. Have an assistant move the mic around the source, and listen carefully to the differences. Sometimes moving the mic back further may give you the sound you are seeking. In film, the sound is fairly natural because the mic is an equal distance away from all sources, and the same mic is used for all sources, so there is some room ambience inherent.

Keep the mic as close to the subject as possible for best audio.

For example, take a scene in an empty warehouse. Our eyes tell us that we should be hearing somewhat boomy, echoing audio. But if the recordist were to use close mic techniques, the room would be substantially de-emphasized, and might create a sense of falseness. Of course, it's possible to create an artificial ambience, and sometimes that has to be done. But, working with the audio that's in the room is usually better than trying to fix it in post. Another example might be a shot in a bathroom made of tile. Our eyes tell us to expect a short echo and a little muddiness in the shot. Consider where the listener is sup-

A mic close to subject in a wide shot may hide the "vast-ness" of a large warehouse, by preventing any of the sound from the room from being recorded. Give the mic a little more distance than usual if you'd like to record some of the room, or record the room to a second channel.

In a tighter shot/frame, the sound of the room may not be as desirable, since the size of the room isn't visible. Recording one close mic and one distanced mic at the same time offers options in post-production.

posed to be. What would it sound like if the listener were a part of the conversation taking place in the shot? Even if it were just a little boy talking to a tree, what would the tree be hearing? How would it sound from the tree's perspective?

Learning to imagine the perspective of the "listener" or receiver of the dialog will tremendously assist you in locating the mic. This technique is much more related to dramatic works rather than interview works, but at the same time, distance and impact should be a consideration in interviews or corporate work.

You might have an interview with a female VP of a major corporation. It could be that close micing gives too much intimacy, or too much breath. If the voice is too breathy, it gives a sense of weakness, or in some cases, a sound that is entirely too personal for the particular scenario you're recording. As a safeguard, consider using the second channel in your camera to record with a distance mic. It's virtually impossible to mess up the audio if you have a close mic and a distance mic recording to separate channels, if both mic levels are properly set during recording.

Ambient Micing: Sometimes referred to as "remote" micing, this is a technique used to pick up more of the room than the actual performance or dialog. This is used to capture the area around the room, reflections of the room, or to produce cutaway sound. This is a great way to record when the camera is a distance away on an extreme wide shot. Generally, this sort of technique infuses the necessary feel of distance in these sorts of scenarios.

Stereo Micing: This is an easy one to get wrong when working with two separate mics. It can be exceptionally simple, but can also be exceptionally difficult. Remember the 4 to 1 rule? Keep the distance if you are close to the source.

If you are looking to record a band for instance, and want a stereo recording, there are a couple of methods in which this can be achieved.

Ambient mic

Direct mic

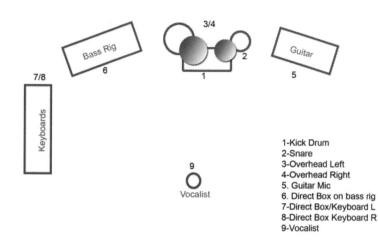

1-Kick Drum
2-Snare
3-Overhead Left
4-Overhead Right
5. Guitar Mic
6. Direct Box on bass rig
7-Direct Box/Keyboard L
8-Direct Box Keyboard R
9-Vocalist

One method is to tap into the band's mixing console. However, if it's a small ensemble and only certain instruments are mic'd, this won't work because only the instruments with microphones will be heard, and they'll be out of balance. You'll do better if you step back to at little past halfway into the room where the blend of instruments is likely more balanced. For a more solid bass in your recording, you'll want to consider a fixed spacing that is one-quarter the 150Hz wavelength (the lowest point source frequency) so, your maximum width would be 24 inches.

Omnidirectional or Cardioid mics work equally well for stereo micing in a large room, with the exception that a Cardioid pattern will not have as good a bottom end/bass due to the proximity effect. Beyond about 3' from the sound source, the mic will be somewhat thin sounding. You might prefer this sound, depending on what else is going into the mix. Personally I prefer working with Omni-directional mics for large room, stereo spreads. It's sometimes humorous to see concert tapers spending a lot of time getting their mics set, fussing over inches in a big area. It makes no difference whatsoever in most situations where they are far back from the stage and sound system. If the speakers on the stage are 15-25 feet apart, then space your mics at approximately the same distance, and slightly back from the center of the room. Doing so will give a blend of room ambience and the speakers. It will generally give you the most natural sound, similar to what you are hearing without headphones. Getting the mics high in the air, as long as they're not close to the ceiling, is usually a good idea, because it somewhat lessens the noise of the crowd and should result in a slightly higher quality recording.

One word of caution about this type of micing; if you ever plan on mixing the stereo signal to mono is that you will possibly experience a "shimmering" or waterfall sound at some frequencies. This is due to similar sounds striking the two mics at slightly different times.

One way to avoid this is to put the two mics as close together as possible so that the ends are on a cross-matched vertical axis. This is known as "coincident" micing.

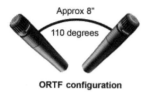

Approx 8"
110 degrees

ORTF configuration

"X-Y" configuration

This is almost the opposite of the stereo technique described above, as the above technique defines stereo by differences in time, whereas the coincident (sometimes called "X-Y") technique defines the stereo space by differences in sound level. Coincident micing is commonly used for close mic techniques. Angles between 120 degrees and never wider than 180 degrees are most common. The Rodé NT4 offers a fixed 90 degree opening, and offers a very sweet close in stereo sound. There are usually no issues with downmixing the stereo audio from coincident recordings to mono.

Any time a director, cameraman, or other person in charge of some aspect of the shoot suggests that you fix it in post, consider quitting right then and there. They wouldn't accept poor lighting and attempt to fix it in post, they wouldn't accept a tear in wardrobe, and attempt to fix it in post, and the same goes for sound. Get it right, or as close to right as humanly possible on the set, and you'll have far less to do in post.

Baffled/Gobo Stereo: This is a fairly rare technique, as it creates an extreme stereo image, but is a good choice for large rooms. What happens in this technique is that the baffle reflects the off-axis sounds, thereby attenuating them. This causes a tremendous sense of separation. The material used for the baffle should be acoustically absorbent using a material such as the sound baffle foam manufactured by companies like Auralex. If the material used for the baffle is reflective, it will likely negatively color the sound hitting the microphone elements. Omni-directional mics are most commonly used for this technique. Cardioid mics can be used, but due to the proximity effect, they will not allow for lower frequencies.

As you can see, microphone placement is critical if you want to achieve the best possible recording. Knowing the microphone types takes you a step closer in achieving that goal.

Lambs wool over a cardboard or foam core disc using omnidirectional mics (AT 4049 pictured)

Chapter 4

Recording, Levels and All

Recording is an art, the basics of which, let alone the intricacies, many people recording today have never taken the time to learn. Getting audio to tape or hard drive isn't as easy as it seems, and this is why there are professional sound people in every walk of the industry. Audio recorded too quietly means that there is more opportunity for noise, even in today's digital workflow. Audio recorded too loud will distort in the analog world, and will simply "brick wall" in digital terms. Unlike Humpty-Dumpty, all the king's horses and all the king's men can't put brick walled audio together again. Getting it right is the best recipe for a successful production.

Once the mics and cables are connected to the camera or other recording device, you'll first want to check levels. There are two kinds of levels; average and peak. Most folks only check for the average, and get the audio too hot (loud). A videographer will step to the camera, and the subject to "say something." This is what they use to test their levels. This is great, assuming the subject will be fairly flat with no speaking dynamics. But if the subject is going to have any kind of rise in their voice, or if the sound will have conversant changes, then all that has been measured using this method, is the average.

What we really need to know is the peak level of the audio, the loudest point the sound will measure under normal circumstances. Therefore, observing more than a "say something" or a "test 1, 2, 3" is important to knowing what the actual level will be. Get your subject to speak in the same manner as they'll be speaking when the recorder/camera is on.

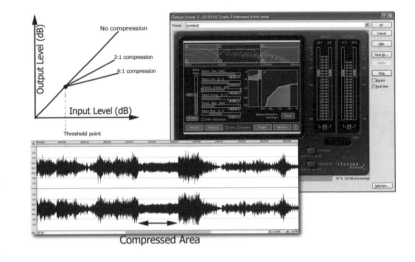

Compressed Area

VU meter   PPM Meter

Most camcorders have meters on them that are based on dBFS, or Decibel Full Scale. This is how digital devices should be calibrated, and usually are. However, some are calibrated logarithmically, (good) and others are calibrated linearly (not so good). Looking at the meter is the only way that are able to tell the difference. If the numbers are "stacked" where the distance appears to be greater as you reach the 0dB point, the meter is logarithmic. If the numbers appear to be the same distance apart regardless of where they are on the meter, it's likely linear. It's important to know how your meter is calibrated, because if you're like most, you'll be looking at meter indicators and not the numbers associated with the meter indicators.

Other chapters have described the audio card, microphone, and cables needed to plug in to the computer or camera. Therefore, assuming all connections are in order, you'll want to boot your NLE or DAW, and get started recording.

You can download test tones from the VASST website if you'd like a calibrated tone to measure your meters in your NLE or camera: http://www.vasst. com/.

Depending on the NLE or DAW, it may have indicators or markers at the 12dB point. Software manufacturers tend to feel this is a good average for recording, and in many cases, it is. However, extreme dynamics, such as those from a passionate speech or maybe from a pulpit pounder, might be too high an average. The goal is to get the recording peaks no louder than -3dB. If this means the average needs to be as low as -18dB, that's OK. The peak is the key. Keep in mind, recording at levels higher than -3dB leaves you no room for processing, and may create problems when it comes time to mix, depending on the content. The other side is a problem too; if signals are recorded too quietly, there won't be enough signal to noise ratio, and the recording will be noisy. Noise is always present in all recording situations.

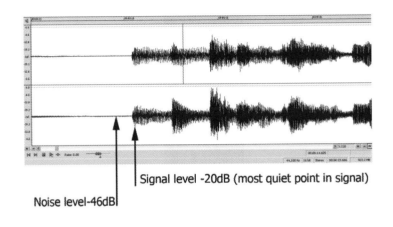

Signal level -20dB (most quiet point in signal)

Noise level-46dB

Whether the noise is generated by electrical sources, from room ambient noise, from a low-quality sound card, or from the mic electronics, noise is a constant factor in all recordings. If the signal to noise ratio is high enough, it's usually very easy to remove a large chunk of the noise in post-processing. It's also likely that if the signal to noise level is high enough, the noise floor will be well below the threshold of hearing at normal mix levels. This is the goal.

One tremendous benefit of the digital environment; noise is never induced in the processing of audio. Once the audio signal has been converted to bits, there no longer is any chance of noise getting into the audio. In the analog world, each processor the audio is routed through inserts noise into the audio flow. Process the audio with enough signal processing, and even slightly unmatched levels, and soon you've got a noise floor that is next to impossible to remove. In the digital world, once it's in the computer, it's very easy to keep the audio clean, particularly with processing plug in tools that offer meters for instant feedback on what is being done to the audio levels.

Now that we understand where averages should lie, let's get signal flowing to the system. In a dialog world, strive for an average of around -12dB. Amateur voice-over artists will likely have a large dynamic range, whereas more seasoned voice-over artists will rarely have more than about 8dB difference in their modulation. Pay attention to newscasters, and you'll generally hear very little dynamic change, even though it might feel like there is a broad dynamic range.

If you're recording your own voice, it's a good practice to speak while looking at the meters, as this will help you discover where your own dynamic range falls into place.

Many systems offer three-colored meters. Generally these are green, yellow, and then red. Green often runs from infinite to -6 or -8dB, and yellow begins at -6 to -8dB on the scale.

Most meters are calibrated to show red at the -3dB point, or somewhere in that range. If the meters were calibrated to only show red at 0dB, then you'd never see red until it was too late to do anything about it, so most systems are calibrated to warn you before the signal is too hot.

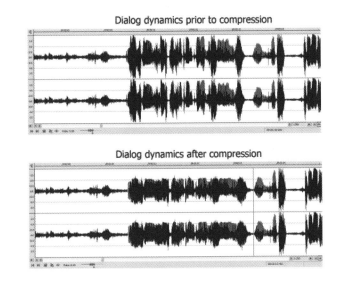

Dialog dynamics prior to compression

Dialog dynamics after compression

Sampling Rates:

More likely than not, your NLE or DAW can record at a variety of sampling rates. The most common is 44.1K/16 bit and 48K/16 bit.

If the audio signal is too low, there is less information for the system to process, and the audio may have aliasing. This is somewhat like a photograph that is too low in resolution.

The way audio is sampled during recording is a given number of slices (sampling frequency) in a given space of time. In the CD world, the audio is sampled 44,100 times per second. Digital video samples the audio at 48,000 times per second. CD and DV audio is given 16 bits, while high-end recording systems record at 24 bits. Greater bit depth offers the ability to record greater dynamic ranges. Greater bit depth is more important overall than the sampling rate, because while the human ear can only hear up to about 15KHz (normal hearing range up to 35 years of age), the sampling rate only needs be twice that of the capability of the human ear. Our ears can perceive tremendous shifts in dynamics, much more so than differences in frequencies.

Greater bit depth means how many "levels" the audio can be sliced. The more bits, the greater the resolution because more information can be contained. So, bit depth is related to the measured quantity of the incoming audio, and sampling frequency is related to the resolution of that amplitude.

Simply put, sample rate is how OFTEN you sample and bit depth is how MUCH you sample each time.

Controlling Levels:

Most NLEs and DAWs offer the ability to control the gain of the incoming signal from the microphone or other sound-generating device. However, some do not. You'll want to be familiar with how to adjust incoming levels if your sound card or system doesn't offer input volume control. In the Microsoft Windows Control Panel, and usually in the system tray, you'll find a Sounds Controller icon.

You can use this to set levels. If your DAW or NLE doesn't offer meters for recording levels, you can download a free Vintage VU meter from PSP software: http://www.pspaudioware.com/start/mix.html. This plug in works for both Apple and Windows applications.

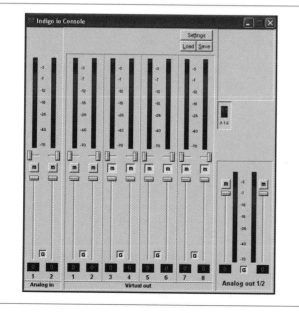

Distortion can be induced at a couple of points in the recording chain, whether digital or analog.

If you are using a sound card with a preamp, you have a couple points of control over the audio. There is an input level to the preamp such as the one you see here on the Echo Audio EchoFire interface. This controls the level at which the microphone is processed through the preamp, and controls the output level of the pre-amplifier. From that point, the audio goes through Echo's software mixer, and from there, to the NLE system. If for example, the preamp is turned too high, and the levels in either the software mixer or the NLE mixer are too low, distortion may be induced in the preamp, but with the levels too low in the NLE, you might not hear that distortion, but it's there.

It's a good idea to leave the software mixer presets in place, and control the audio from the mic preamplifier, rather than trying to use the software to control the input/output.

In some cases, such as my personal studio, I leave my John Hardy pre-amps set to an average point for most recording, but control the input levels to Sony Vegas using the Vegas gain control by way of the Mackie Universal Control.

Rather than using a microphone pre-amp, you might want to consider using an external mixer, whose outputs feed either the internal sound card or a professional external sound card. Using a mixer will also allow several sound generating devices such as CD players, DVD players, tape machines, various mics, keyboards, or other input device to be recorded by the computer without having to patch various devices into a sound card.

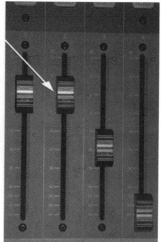

Unity gain indicators are found on nearly all mixing devices.

In this case, set the faders on the mixer to Unity Gain, usually indicated by brackets on most mixers, and then use the mixer's gain control to set levels for program input. Download the 0dB test tone from the VASST website and play it through the mixer. Adjust the gain controls and set the mixer controls to 0dB, with all channels at Unity Gain. Set the gain controls on the mixer until the mixer's meters read exactly 0dB. This lets you know where 0dB lies within your mixer. You should do the same thing with the downloadable -12dB sound file, adjusting the mixer's outputs to -12dB. Test this with the meters in your computer.

Keep in mind that all analog mixers may generate noise at every stage in the audio chain. Therefore, keep EQ's bypassed, keep aux feeds turned off, and keep any FX sends turned off, unless you are using them. Some mixers have switches to disable these features; others merely need to be turned to the null, or zero point. Remember that you can always do noise-free equalization, reverb, compression, and other processes inside your DAW or NLE system, so you're best to do any processing there, if you can. Sometimes you may need compression or other processing to take place in the audio chain before the audio signal hits the hard drive, and while this is fine, it's important to remember that every device in the chain prior to the hard drive will introduce noise into the signal. Just how much noise depends on the quality of the equipment and the gain stages in the signal flow.

In this image, you can see the difference between a high noise floor and a lower noise floor. Keep in mind that noise is virtually always present. The question boils down to how much noise is acceptable.

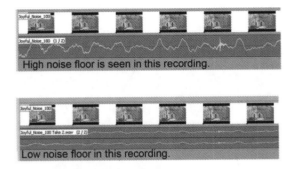

High noise floor is seen in this recording.

Low noise floor in this recording.

Same project, same recording time, but the lower recording was done using an Echo Layla 3G card, whereas the upper recording is via a standard computer sound card. If professional-quality audio is your goal, you'll need a higher quality sound card than what comes with the average computer system.

Chapter 5

Understanding Analog vs Digital Metering

Taking Measure: Metering

You wouldn't build a house without a tape measure, and you likely wouldn't bake a cake without a measuring cup. Measuring audio levels is critical in the digital domain, and displays called "meters" provide the measuring tools we need in order to ascertain audio levels.

In order to know what relative volume is in the audio world, virtually all applications offer some sort of metering. Unfortunately, all meters are not measured equally. Meters come in different types, and levels of measurement, and are even different for the analog world versus the digital world.

In the digital domain, most applications offer Volume Unit or "VU" meters. These meters are fine for average performance, and are what most folks familiar with audio tools will recognize immediately. In the analog world, VU meters are thin needles that move from one side to the other, providing measurement information. Although these provide good information about the average levels and dynamics of audio being measured, they do not provide accurate information that can be counted upon in the digital realm.

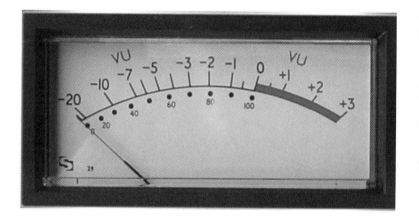

A properly calibrated VU meter has a rise time of 300 ms, and this is far too slow for the digital world when working with hot levels and close tolerances. How is the rise level determined? If a 1KHz tone at 0dB is applied to a properly calibrated VU meter, then it should take 300ms for the indicator to reach and stay at the zero dB point on the meter; by the same token, it should take 300ms for the indicator to fall.

When I was younger, I once heard Tom Stockham (father of digital audio) refer to the VU meter as "Virtually Useless." Later on in life, this became a fairly common term. And for digital use in particular, VU meters are effectively useless, even in software form. Why? Because they are weighted for an average of the audio signal, and the peaks in the signal could very easily be well beyond the 0dB point but the recording engineer might never know it. Any transient sound, such as a snare drum or other fast attack/decay instrument would barely move the VU meter, due to its slow response times. VU meters work very well on constant sounds, but transients, which are a huge part of most audio programming, can't accurately be measured in this nearly 100-year old measuring tool. And to make matters a bit more challenging, few analog VU meters are actually accurate, and in most cases, haven't been calibrated to spec.

VU meters are sometimes referred to as "analog meters" even though VU metering is often found in the digital domain.

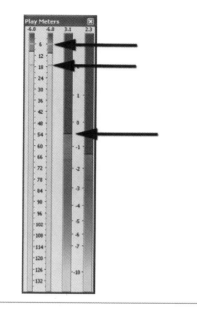

The Peak Meter

The Peak Meter, otherwise known as the PPM or Peak Programming Meter, is a standard in the digital and analog industry. Standard in that it provides accurate information about the peaks of the audio signal, but interestingly enough, there is no standard scale to the meter other than marking where the 0dB and other relevant levels exist. The biggest difference between a VU meter and a PPM meter is the velocity of the metering. A correctly calibrated PPM meter should have a 10ms rise time. This is significantly faster than the 300ms rise time of the VU meter! However, in order to allow the meter to be comprehended, the fall time of the meter is significantly slower than the VU meter. Notice in this image that there are actually 3 levels indicated in the PPM meter (left) and the VU meter (right). The PPM meter shows both peaks and valleys, while the VU meter is showing the averaging of the signal.

Virtually all NLE and DAW systems offer a PPM or Peak meter in the application. Some offer both, and most offer various levels of meter scaling. Meter scaling will vary slightly from one geographic region to another, so if you're working with super critical levels, be sure you know to which scale your software meters are calibrated. In truth, meters aren't some standardized, locked in scale that you must adhere to at every turn. Think of them more like a speedometer on a vehicle that provides very accurate feedback, but doesn't govern your every move.

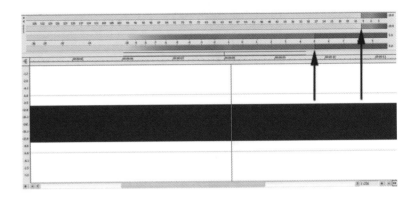

Notice that the meters are responding differently to the -10dB signal being fed to them; check the averaging level in the VU meter in this type of meter, vs the analog modeling meters shown.

PPM/Peak meters are often referred to as "digital meters" but this isn't really accurate, as there are devices in the analog world such as the Dorrough meters that offer PPM metering with analog input.

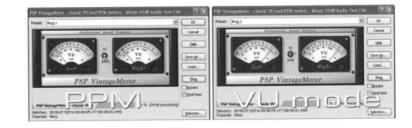

Why Do I Care?

Analog recording/playback levels are somewhat flexible; 0dB only serves as an averaging level but doesn't act like a governor or anything of the sort. In fact, some analog recording tape is designed specifically to allow for signals much hotter than 0dB, sometimes going as hot as +12dB!

In the digital realm, 0dB is the maximum level. After 0dB, there is no more. A simple way to consider what is often referred to as "hitting the brick wall" is to understand that once your signal has hit 0dB, it's gone, shattered like an egg that hit that brick wall, and no amount of superglue can bring it back to its pristine state prior to being shattered.

So, where audio could have peaks in the 0dB range and go as much as +4dB over in the analog world before anyone noticed much, digital isn't quite as forgiving. In fact, it's a good idea to never have maximum levels greater than -2dB from a digital source, just in case the listener/viewer of your media has older oversampling systems that could distort if the signal is too hot.

The problem lies in matching the currently analog world of broadcast, such as Beta SP machines and their counterparts, to the digital realm. Many broadcast engineers or duplication houses will still use the test tone from a digital source tape to calibrate their meters, thereby setting the loudness for the peaks of a project. Except that most broadcast machines use VU meters and digital gear generally use peak metering.

Now, the industry has determined that -20dBFS (decibel-full scale) is the standard setting for nominal values for broadcasting audio. Fine and well. Understand that if you are using most NLE systems, a -20dB signal won't even draw a line in your audio window, and you can't see what's going on. As an editor, you'll want to know what's going on. It's important to recognize that this might be the industry standard, but we set mix levels for music somewhat hotter in the studio at approximately -6dB from 0dBfs, and worry about output volume at the end of the project, just prior to printing to a master tape destined to make a transition from the digital to analog realm. Remember, if the media is staying in the digital realm, you never need to worry, so long as it never crosses 0dBFS.

Given that peak dynamic ranges of processed digital signals average to peak around 15db above 0VU, set the test tone at -20dB, and leave it at that. This provides extra headroom in the event of a large dynamic spike. To further safeguard audio, in the final process/print to tape, insert a compressor with a soft limit at -3dB. This assures that the signal will never cross 0dBfs. A hard limiter could also be used set to -1.5 dB, but if the audio is too hot, when the limiter is slammed, it will clearly be heard and possibly muddy the sound.

It's important to remember that the s/n ratio is approximately 6dB different in analog to digital comparisons. In other words, an analog tape will sound 6dB louder than it's digital counterpart when calibrated to the same peak level. So there is nothing actually lost, and preserving signal integrity is clearly more critical than s/n ratio.

The challenge comes when studios, equipped with DAT machines or other mechanical digital devices look at their meters. The meters on digital devices may be calibrated to -20dBFS, -18dBFS, and -14dBFS translating to 0VU. However, uncompressed, or live media can easily cover the narrower dynamic ranges, and cross the dreaded line of no return and mashed bits.

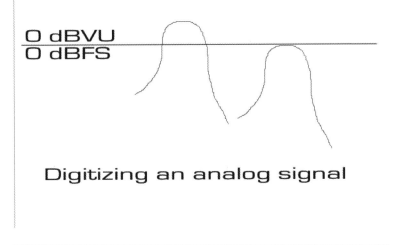

Digitizing an analog signal

However, "where do I take my reference level from? average or peak measurements?" is continually asked. In the digital world, it's not so much where you take the level from, but it is critical you know what that level IS. By making sure that signals have less than 18dB of dynamic range through the use of a compressor, and by making sure that PEAK levels are less than 0dBFS, then there should be no issue at print. This is why we recommend the use of plugins like the Izotope and WAVES Ultramaximizer. Sony has a tool known as "WaveHammer" that comes with Sound Forge and Vegas as well.

There are also a large number of metering packages available from several different manufacturers. Some are free, such as those from PSP Audioware, and others are paid-for packages such as those available from Universal Audio or Elemental Audio Systems. For Apple users, SpectraFoo is one of the standards in the industry.

As you record dialog, it's a good idea to keep the average level of the dialog at approximately -12dB. As other sounds are recorded, be sure peaks don't cross -3dB in the recording process, and being a bit lower is acceptable. You want to be sure to keep levels hot, rather than low however, because if levels are low, you'll affect the resolution of the file.

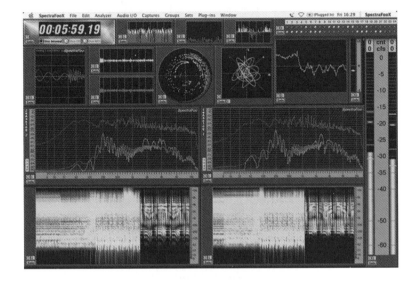

Chapter 6

Connecting Microphones to a Camcorder

There are some things to know when connecting a microphone (or microphones) to a camcorder. Things such as what kind of connection the microphone uses and how to adapt to a situation where the microphone and camera's connectors do not match, makes all the difference.

Low Impedance vs. High Impedance

Low impedance, or balanced connections, provide protection against interference and noise. Low impedance connections can be run great distances for hundreds of feet and not have any degradation in the signal. An example of a low impedance connection is XLR, commonly found on microphones and professional-level audio gear.

High impedance, or unbalanced connections, are not protected against noise like balanced connections are. High impedance connections typically cannot be run for very long distances, typically around 18-20 feet at maximum; they become like an instant radio antenna, conducting a lot of noise. An example of a high impedance connection is 1/4" tip-sleeve, or TS.

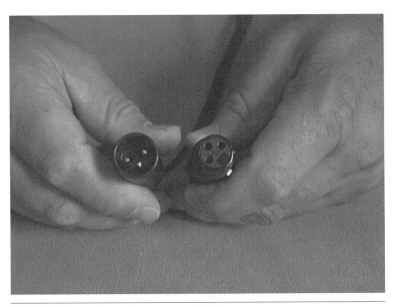

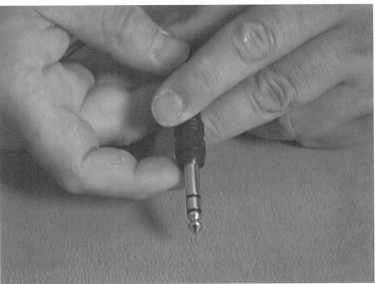

Most pro-level cameras use an XLR jack to input audio. Most consumer and prosumer-level cameras use the 3.5 mm (or 1/8") stereo minijack connector.

If the latter is the case, you can use an XLR to 3.5 mm minijack adapter to connect a mic with an XLR connector to the 3.5 mm input on your camera. XLR to 3.5 mm stereo minijack adapters should be very short.

Thread the adapter cable around the handle or under the camera's own mic before you plug it into the camera's input so that it doesn't get in the way.

Wireless Systems

Wireless systems operate much like wired systems, with the exception, naturally, of the wireless connection made between the receiver (which goes to the camera) and the transmitter (which goes to the microphone). (For more tips on what wireless systems to use, see Chapter 15, "Understanding Wireless Systems.")

You typically plug in the output of the wireless receiver to the camera's input using a 3.5 mm to 3.5 mm cable. The microphone plugs into the transmitter.

Alternative Connection Formats

For situations where the mic needs to be a great distance from the camera, devices such as Beachtek's DXA8 will convert a low impedance XLR signal to a high impedance 3.5 mm stereo minijack signal right into the camera. In addition, this device provides other features such as phantom power (for condenser microphones such as shotgun mics), volume controls and even a limiter. This type of device also has the benefit of more than one mic input.

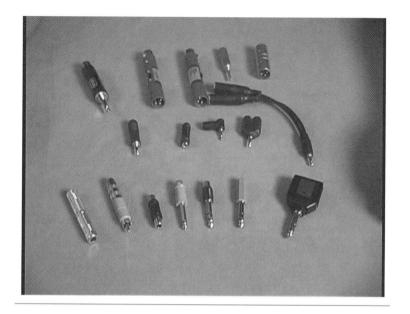

There are literally hordes of different adapter plugs and cables out there just in case you need to convert one type of connection (like XLR) into another connection type (like 3.5 mm). As a general rule of thumb, always keep a large collection of adapters and cables handy. You never know when you may need them. You can keep them in padded lunchboxes (available from any department store) labeled with gaffer's tape so that you know what's in the bag.

As you can see, connecting a microphone to a camcorder is not that straightforward a task, but the task is made easier if you know beforehand what to expect.

Chapter 7

Effective Mic Boom Techniques

It's a fact that the closer you are to the sound source you intend to record, the better the audio and less editing you'll have to do down the road. This chapter outlines some techniques and tips on using boom mics for such a task.

Length of Boompole

The length of the boompole is generally dependent on the type of production. Poles for commercial projects like TV, commercials or feature films typically range from 12 to 15 feet. Documentary-style projects like you see on reality TV and the news typically range from 5 to 8 feet. However, booms can be much longer. Some booms, like this image of the K-Tek ENG boom, are articulated, and may bend in the middle.

When you use the boom, do not extend the boompole to its maximum at the safety stops. Instead, extend the pole all the way and then bring it back a couple inches. Not only will this prevent the pole from wilting, it will be quieter too. Quiet is important.

Another good tip is to extend the pole further than what is needed so that the boompole will counterbalance itself in your hands. Holding a boom for long periods of time can cause muscle strain, so any balance advantage is beneficial.

Boom the Mic from Above

Booming the mic from above provides several advantages and is usually the best option most of the time. It will give you the best audio possible since the source you intend to record is closer to the mic rather than several feet away using a camera mic or shotgun mic. The "line of sight" for the mic will be towards the subject and then towards the ground. Whatever sound the subject produces will dominate the soundtrack and any ambient noise in the background serves to fully texturize the scene being filmed.

Boom the Mic from Below

Sometimes, booming the mic from below may be an option best taken when booming from above cannot be done due to too many obstructions. Note that booming from underneath is usually difficult in terms of composition of shot (showing a actor's torso makes more sense than showing an actor's head and some empty air above).

Noise from Cables

Cable noise is usually caused by several problems, including percussion, loose connections and conductance.

Conductance is noise that travels along the sheath of the pole due to physical vibrations. Boompoles, like the RoboPole, have a compressed foam-encapsulated cable that runs the entire length of the inside section.

Percussion happens when the cable bangs against the remaining sections of the boompole. Since boompoles are telescopic, it's not possible to foam-dampen any tube but the innermost tube. Holding the cable taut while holding the boom can prevent percussion; as the cable exits from the boom, loop the cable around your thumb or little finger. You don't want the cable to merely exit the boom and drop to the floor.

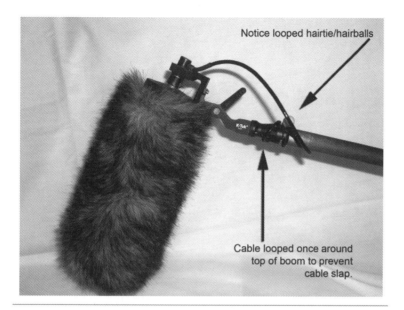

Notice looped hairtie/hairballs

Cable looped once around
top of boom to prevent
cable slap.

The mic connection can also be a source of noise, as XLR connections can loosen from repeated use. Placing a strip of cloth camera tape over the connection between where the mic and boom meet will help prevent a spotty connection while the mic is moved around. Always keep some slack in the connection between the mic and the boom. Any excess cable should be wrapped around the pole beneath the shockmount once (or twice).

A useful tip is to use a short jumper cable inside of the blimp windscreens. This cable should terminate at the handle of the shockmount, and be permanently attached with cable ties or tape. This will help simplify the process of mounting the shockmount to the pole, because it will no longer be necessary to open up the windscreen and dress the cable every time you need to use the mic.

Holding the Boom

When holding a boom, you'll want to hold it so that fatigue is minimized. This is achieved by holding the boom as if you were about to start a pull-up; keep your arms close but extended all the way vertically, with the elbows locked (but not tight).

Use your front arm as a prop to support the boompole above your body. If possible, handle the boom at its natural balance point, with your rear arm to pan, steer, or tilt.

Position of Mic

You'll want to position the mic so that it's as close to the action as allowed, as the sound from the subject being recorded will be clear and distinct rather than muddled and poor. When placing the mic, dip the mic completely into the camera shot, and then slowly raise the mic until the camera operator tells you that you're just barely clear.

In closing, boom mic positioning and technique is essential to capturing the audio as pristinely as possible. These tips and techniques are hopefully beneficial for you.

Chapter 8

Monitoring Audio on a Production

Monitoring audio is a very important aspect of your project. Audio is 70% of a what viewer "sees" when watching a video. It's obvious that the audio should be the best that it can possibly be. This chapter outlines some tips on what to look for in audio monitors, as well as some pointers on using headphones in the field.

Monitors

Monitors are one of the most important aspects of your NLE or DAW setup, as they allow you to hear the audio that's in your project with great accuracy.

You might think you're just ducky with those inexpensive, plastic computer speakers that came with your system (illustrated here), but guess what? They're not great for monitoring, if at all. If you're at all serious about your audio, you're much better off springing for a decent pair of monitors. They range in price from $199 a pair to $1,000 or more for a single monitor.

There are essentially two kinds of monitors: Active and passive. Active monitors are provided with an amplifier, while passive monitors do not have one and require a separate amplifier to drive them.

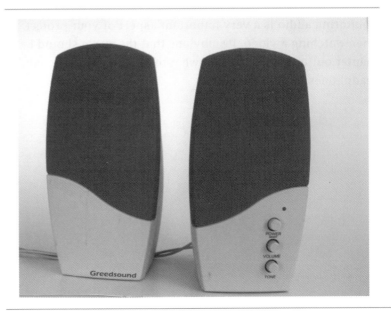

Active monitors, though more expensive due to being driven by their own amplifier, are the better choice for a couple of reasons: They have an amplifier that is matched, or tuned, to the monitor. Also, having monitors that are already driven also means less cabling; you don't have to run cables from your computer (or mixer) to the amplifier to the monitor in an active monitor setup. As a result, active monitors are more common than their passive cousins.

There are quite a few brands out there to choose from. Genelec (http://www.genelec.com), M-Audio (http://www.m-audio.com), and Mackie (http://www.mackie.com) are just a few companies that produce great monitors.

Just about all pro-quality monitors come with both XLR and 1/4 inch TRS (tip-ring-sleeve) inputs. Where possible, use the XLR inputs.

Positioning

Monitors should be placed at least six inches or more away from the wall and equidistant to each other and to you, the listener. If the monitors are four feet apart, then they should be four feet from you. The monitors' should also be facing you at an angle rather than straight ahead at an opposing wall.

You will want to mount the monitors on a isolation pads like those from Auralex. (http://www.auralex.com) This is so the monitors are separated from your desk (effectively decoupling them from the desk) so as to not color the sound.

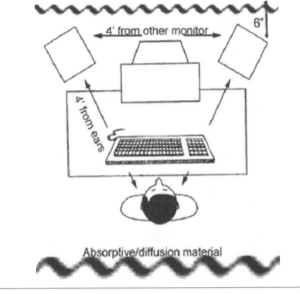

MoPAD Monitor Isolation Pads

Similarly, you will want to eliminate reflections and room bounce; this is critical in order to hear what's going on in your mix. A simple blanket hung on the wall won't cut it; it'll only cut out very high frequencies but not much else. Companies like Auralex also make special materials for this very purpose, usually for a nominal price.

Auralex has a Web site called, "Auralex University," where you can obtain information on how to best set up your room acoustically. More info can be found at: http://www.auralexuniversity.com

Whatever you do, DO NOT use material like egg crate foam that is used for mattresses. It breaks down quickly and creates more dust as well as particles in your listening area. On top of that, it can be a fire hazard, invalidating your insurance. Spend the extra cash for proper elimination of room bounce.

Subwoofers

Most monitors have really good reproduction of bass frequencies, but if you really want to feel the bass, especially when monitoring a soundtrack, you might want to spring for a subwoofer. Most monitors have a matching subwoofer that you can buy separately to add that extra oomph.

One important thing to mention is that if you intend to mix for 5.1 surround, get a subwoofer that has a discrete input, rather than a subwoofer that requires you to plug your satellites (the monitors) directly into the subwoofer. This is so the LFE (low frequency enclosure) channel is not affected by anything that's happening in the satellites.

> **Satellites are simply monitors that act as the extension of the subwoofer. They take care of the higher frequencies while the subwoofer (typically) takes care of the frequencies 250Hz and below.**

> **The low frequency enclosure, or LFE, channel is simply the subwoofer channel. Most NLE and DAW software programs refer to the subwoofer channel as the LFE channel.**

Another thing to look for in a subwoofer is a tunable crossover frequency control, one that allows you to set at least 250Hz or below.

Similar to active monitors, it's highly recommended that subwoofers have their own amplifier; subwoofers typically need a lot of power to operate. Whatever subwoofer you choose, make sure it's at least three times the power of whatever your satellites are.

If you're just going to do stereo, having the subwoofer power the satellites will work just fine. Some monitoring systems, like M-Audio's LX4 5.1 Expander System, let you transform the LX4 2.1 System into a fully surround-capable system.

Connecting a subwoofer is usually a simple affair. Instead of connecting your computer or mixer (or other sound source) to the satellites, you connect the computer or mixer's output to the subwoofer's input. The subwoofer then has discrete outputs for the satellites.

Subwoofers usually come with a crossover frequency control, also called a low pass frequency (LPF) control, that lets you decide what the highest frequency will be that the subwoofer will reproduce. Because of room size and other variables (such as subwoofer position relative to a wall), there's no magic number to use. Generally, a good starting point is about 250 Hz or lower.

Subwoofers also typically have a crossover frequency control, also called a high pass frequency (HPF) control, that lets you decide what the lowest frequency will be that the satellites will reproduce. Generally speaking, if your listening environment is optimally set up, it should be set the same as the subwoofers LPF setting.

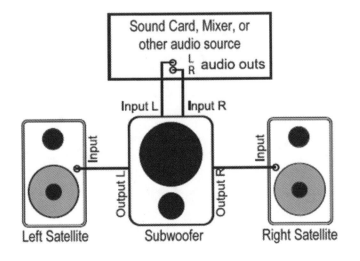

The positioning of subwoofers is not terribly important, since bass is basically nondirectional. Note that placing a subwoofer against a wall will increase its bass response.

Headphones

Post-Production

When listening to your audio in post-production, it's great to use headphones when you need to keep the volume down or make quick tweaks, but you'll definitely want to use monitors otherwise.

On the Field

It's critical to monitor the audio at all times while out on the field. You must be able to hear what anomalies (such as wind blowing over the microphone or line noise from bad cables) there are in the audio. The only way to do this is with headphones as it's the only audio connection you have to the microphone. If you can't hear exactly what's coming in, how do you know what you're going to have when you get back to the studio?

There are several types of headphones to use in these situations:

In-the-ear headphones – This type of headphone totally blocks out external sound so that you only hear what's coming in via the microphone. Etymotic Research, Inc. (http://www.etymotic.com) makes a wide range of in-the-ear headphones for you to choose from.

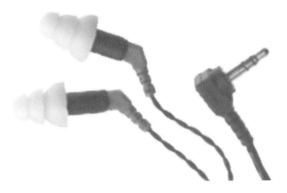

On-the-ear headphones – This type of headphone rests on your ear so that you may hear mostly what's coming from the microphone but also outside the headphones. Sony's (http://bssc.sel.sony.com/BroadcastandBusiness/index.shtml) MDR-7506 is practically the world standard headphone in this class.

Over-the-ear headphones – This type of headphone almost acts like an in-the-ear headphone but instead completely covers your ears for a better acoustical seal to the outside.

Remember that these brands are just guidelines. There are so many makes, models and price ranges; find a head-phone that's right for you.

Chapter 9

Mixing Techniques

Learning how to mix is a science that's far beyond the scope of this book. But if you know what to look for in a mixer, it should come a little more naturally with practice. This chapter outlines what mixer types there are, some tips on using them, and some mixing features available in NLEs.

Mixing in the Field

When mixing in the field, it's obviously best to use a field mixer, which is specifically designed with mixing sound on location in mind.

Field mixers also have some features that are quite useful such as:

- Tone generators, which provide a reference tone for the editor as a constant point of reference at the head of each take or reel.

- High and low cuts and roll-offs, which are handy in eliminating hiss, rumble and other types of noise before it reaches the camera.

- Input peak limiters, which will ensure that the recording levels do not clip.

Field mixers are typically small, rugged and should ideally be battery powered and lightweight. (Some mixers that are portable enough to be used out on the field or in the studio can be powered by both batteries and AC power.) Field mixers can also help quite a bit when you need to input two or more microphones into your camcorder.

On a lot of video shoots, a cameraman might also be the sound person. If this is the case, the mixer being used should have a carry strap with controls that are accessible with markings that are easy to read. The controls should not be prone to being moved if bumped.

Take into consideration how many inputs you will need as well as the input types. Most pro and prosumer mics have the standard XLR connectors, while others have 1/4" TRS and 1/8" stereo mini plugs. You can, of course, use adapters but it's always better to connect directly to the mixer.

Meters on the field mixer are very handy for showing if the input is clipping or not. In addition, field mixers typically have an input peak limiter, which prevents the incoming signal from clipping.

Similar to the inputs, take note of the mixer's outputs and whether or not they match your camcorder's input. Professional cameras have XLR inputs, while consumer and prosumer models only have an 1/8" stereo minijack input. Use adapters as necessary.

Mixing in the Post-Room

For mixers in the post-room, the choices are incredibly vast. A lot of mixers for the studio are small enough to fit on your desktop yet offer the same amount of control and power as their bigger cousins (minus the number of inputs and outputs).

Studio mixers also have EQ controls so you can have some level of control over the highs, mids and lows of your input, as well as panning controls.

A blend of connections are also typical on studio mixers. XLR, 1/4" (either balanced or unbalanced), RCA or a combination of these connections are available for the purposes of connecting different devices such as a CD player (typically via the "tape" or RCA input).

Just like field mixers, studio mixers also have metering capability so that you can ensure the input levels don't clip.

Using a Mixer

A really good studio mixer provides several audio tools to simplify your production duties. As a mixer, it combines multiple sources for video recording, but that isn't its only purpose. You could use your mixer to record voiceovers or sound effects directly into the computer. You could also hire musicians to record original background music, and mix the performance from there. Combined with the appropriate software, your computer and mixer make a great audio production team.

Another great use for your audio mixer is as a level-matching tool. If you use an analog video-capture card, you may have difficulties matching audio levels from different takes, not to mention different sources. Patch the audio from your raw footage tapes via the mixer just before going into the audio capture card. Using the volume and tone controls, it's easy to achieve a good audio balance. In addition, you'll eliminate recaptures due to overloaded signal peaks and save rendering time by applying tone adjustments prior to audio capture.

Using an NLE

Nonlinear editors (and other digital audio workstation applications) contain a
mixer panel of some sort that operates
similarly in function as a real world
mixer minus some features such as
EQ (which is usually done at the track
level or bus level).

In addition, the mixing options available in NLEs allow for complex mixing
and routing capabilities. You could,
for example, route a specific track to a
specific hardware output of your audio
interface via a bus (where you're free
to route anywhere you'd like, such as
an external recorder or mixer). You
could even route a bus to another bus
if you wanted.

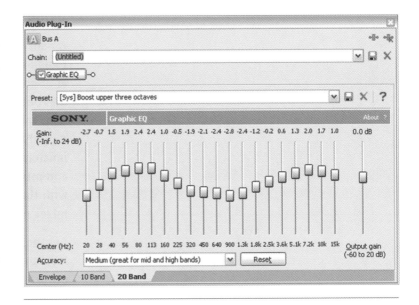

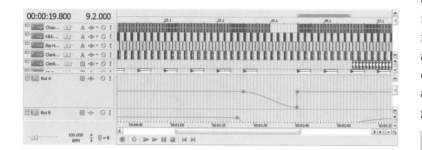

On top of that, you have an enormous amount of control over the audio in an NLE with features such as automatable envelopes. You could, for example, route a group of tracks to a bus, then insert a volume envelope on the bus and slowly make those tracks fade over time. You don't have to sit there and turn a knob in real time; just "program" the NLE to do it for you.

Not every NLE or DAW application has these features; be sure to check your app's documentation for such a feature.

The great thing about NLEs and DAWs is that they're very flexible. You can go back to a particular point in your project and change the routing or mixing without affecting the original audio (unless you commit to changes such as bouncing down a track).

As you can see, there are many options available to you when mixing, whether it is in the field, in the studio or using an NLE or DAW. Explore the avenues available to find your best option.

Chapter 10

Plug-In Tools for Nonlinear Editing Systems

Sometimes, problems can occur with recorded audio that are discovered after the fact. This chapter outlines some plug-ins that can help and some tips on using them.

What Do Plug-Ins Do?

Plug-ins are a software component that work in conjunction with its host program, be it a nonliner editing system (such as Vegas) or a digital audio editor (such as Sound Forge).

Some plug-ins are designed to provide tools that can enhance elements such as digital audio. Some are designed to provide a creative avenue when working with your audio.

Some plug-ins come with an application (like Sony Pictures Digital's XFX series shipped with Vegas, Sound Forge and ACID Pro). Some you buy and install separately. If you buy a plug-in to install, you usually setup the plug-in using its executable (.EXE) file.

There are a few types of plug-in architectures, most notably DirectX (developed by Microsoft) and VST (developed by Steinberg). Most vendors produce DirectX and VST versions of the same plug-in for the most compatibility amongst applications.

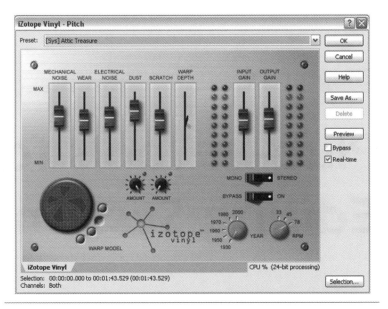

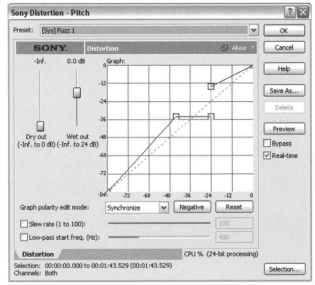

DirectX plug-in installations are usually a simple affair. You simply install the plug-in and open the host application to get cracking at using the plug-in on your audio.

VST plug-in installations require that you place the plug-in's necessary DLL in a folder or location. You then indicate in your host application where the DLL and can then work with the plug-in like you can with DirectX plug-ins.

Which Ones Do I Need?

You'll more than likely want the staples for editing: A compressor, an EQ, a gate, and a reverb. Most software packages come with these types of tools as standard, but the more powerful plug-ins are available for purchase to use with your host application.

Using Compressors, Reverbs, EQ, Gates, and Other Tools

Compressors

A compressor is designed to help add some punch by limiting the dynamic range of your audio. Don't overdo it with a compressor; unnatural, analog-like distortion can result if it's overused.

Typical settings in a compressor include;

Threshold – Sets the level at which the compressor begins acting on the signal

Ratio – Sets the compression ratio of input to output levels. For example, a ratio of 3.5 to 1 means that a signal exceeding the threshold by 3.5 dB will be allowed 1 dB of increased output

Attack – Sets the time required for the compressor to start acting on the signal once the level rises above the threshold. Low attacks preserve percussive sounds; higher attacks cause sounds to slowly swell in volume

Release – Sets the time it takes for the compressor to "shut off" once the level falls below the threshold

Output – Sets the overall output gain after compression

Peak and RMS – Peak mode crushes the signal rising above the threshold, no matter how fast the transient is. RMS mode is a little more forgiving and will allow fast transients through but will clamp down if continuous peaks appear

Hard knee compressors – are the standard type of compressor, and apply the full amount of compression once the level rises above the set threshold.

Soft knee compressors – by comparison, gradually and gently compress the signal until it fully applies its gain reduction at the full level set at the ratio. As a result, soft knee compressors are more suitable for entire mixes.

Reverbs

Reverbs are a creative effect when you want to sweeten your audio and make it sound expansive. Don't overkill it though. You don't want the audio to sound like it's in a cave if the subject is in a small room.

A typical reverb effect plug-in comes with settings that help you tailor the sound you are trying to reproduce.

They are:

Dry out – The amount of unprocessed signal that will be mixed in the final output

Reverb out – The amount of processed signal that will be mixed in the final output

Early reflection style and early out – The amount of "early reflection" that will be mixed into the final output. Early reflections are the first reflections you hear when a sound is created in space and typically only bounce once before you hear them. Your ear uses these first sounds to judge the size of the space.

Decay time – The amount of time it takes for the reverb to decay

Pre-delay – The amount of time it takes between the initial sound of the source of audio and the start of its reverb

Attenuate high and low frequencies (high and low pass filters) – Reverbs tend to attenuate high and low frequencies as they bounce around in space. This setting helps to mimic that phenomenon.

By adjusting the dry out, reverb out and early out, you can make a source sound closer or farther away. For example, by giving more dry out than reverb out, a source will sound closer. Likewise, giving more reverb than dry will make a source sound like it's farther away.

Dull rooms also tend to attenuate frequencies at around 5,000Hz or so. Brighter rooms tend to attenuate frequencies at a higher setting, around 10,000Hz to 15,000Hz. As always, experiment with this setting.

A creative use of reverb is to create a ghostly "reverse reverb" effect. The effect works best on material such as voices, or material that has moments of silence.

To create such an effect in your digital audio editor:

1. Open the file you intend to create the effect on. Reverse the audio using your digital audio editor's reverse command.

2. Apply the reverb effect to the reversed audio. A big, expansive reverb with lots of decay works best.

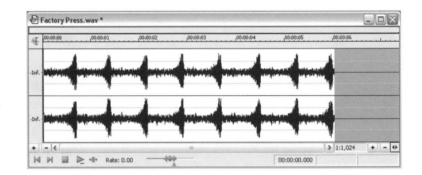

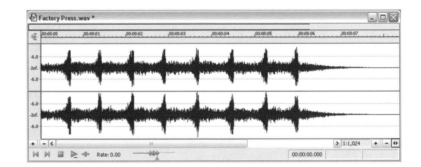

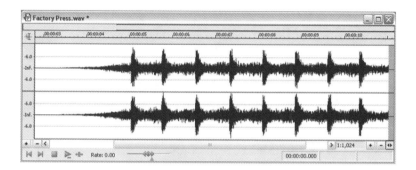

3. Reverse the audio once more. Playback the audio to hear the effect. It should sound like a reversed swell before the actual audio plays back.

Noise Gates

A noise gate simply helps eliminate any buzz that may be present during quiet moments in your audio. You may not use it in every instance, but it's still quite handy all the same.

A noise gate plug-in typically has the following settings:

Threshold – Sets the level at which the noise gate removes the signal. This is typically around -40dB or so

Attack – Amount of time it takes for the noise gate to act once the level rises above the threshold. Lower settings preserve percussive attacks, while higher settings cause the audio to swell in volume

Release – Amount of time it takes for the noise gate to stop once the level sinks below the threshold. Higher settings will preserve decays, while lower settings will cut them off EQs

EQs are used to help boost and cut frequencies in the audio that may need it. Several types of EQ exist: graphic, paragraphic, and parametric.

Graphic EQs divide the frequency range of the audio into several bands of frequencies to tweak to your liking.

Paragraphic EQs provide more control over isolating and cutting and/or boosting specific frequencies. They are actually a hybrid of graphic and parametric EQs.

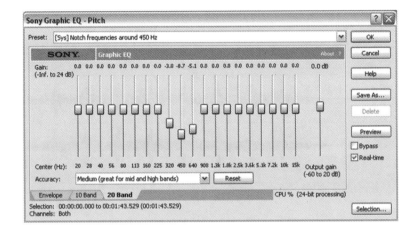

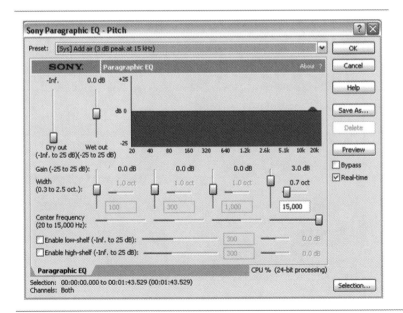

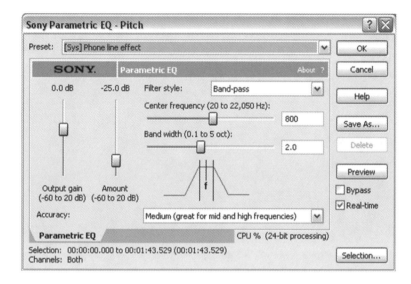

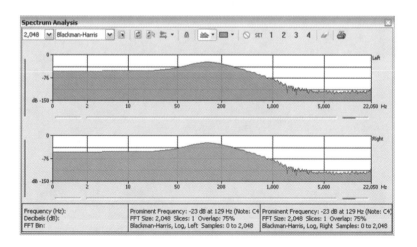

Parametric EQs focus in on a specific frequency to adjust.

There are many other tools such as Sound Forge's Spectrum Analyzer tool, which will let you see at a glance what frequencies are lacking and need to be massaged.

Getting Optimal Voiceovers with Plug-Ins

You know that they say: Garbage in, garbage out. The best way of getting a great voiceover is to have the best optimal recording conditions—a good mic and a good environment in which to record. Still, there are a couple tips and tricks worth mentioning.

Compressor

A great tip to try is to place your audio on one track and your voiceover on the other and have your compressor "duck" your audio behind the voiceover. To do that:

1. Place your voiceover on one track and background audio on the other. Increase your voicover's volume as close to unity (0.0 dBFS) as possible. Decrease your audio track between 7 and 14dB.

2. Insert a compressor on the master bus. Set the Threshold to between -10 to -15dB.

3. Set the Amount to 8:1. Set the Attack to 15ms and Release to 250ms.

4. Playback the project and experiment with the track volumes and compressor settings to find the best combination.

Note that the effect is very subtle but works quite well.

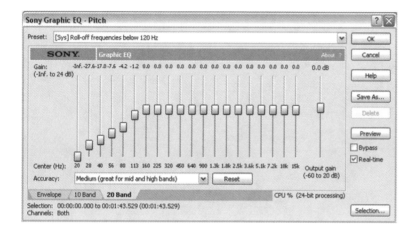

EQ

You'll probably want to use the different forms of EQ to help compensate for any shortcomings your voice or the mic used may have. If the voiceover is too boomy, cut the bass. Similarly, if there's too much brightness, cut the treble frequencies.

Many EQ plug-ins come with presets that help boost or cut specific frequencies. Experiment with these on your audio to get a good idea on what works and what doesn't.

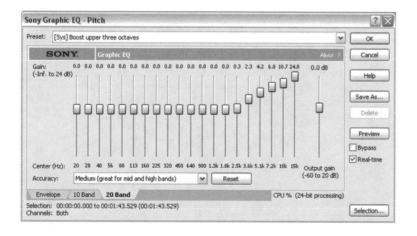

Other Plug-Ins

Other tools which would be useful for voiceovers include VASST's Ultimate S plug-in, which works with Sony Pictures Digital's Vegas 5 and Vegas 6. It has 55 editing and creative functions, including a tool that allows you to easily duck audio behind a voiceover track. More info can be found at: http://www.vasst.com/search.aspx?category=Plugins

Getting Good Field Audio with Plug-Ins

If field audio is giving you trouble, like background noise or hum, Sony Pictures Digital's Noise Reduction 2 DirectX plug-in is a great tool to have. It will help remove background noise while preserving the material you want to keep. For more information, see Chapter 11, "Noise Reduction".

As you can see, there are many plug-in choices out there that will help you enhance your audio. As always, experiment to find the best solution for your needs.

Chapter 11

Noise Reduction

Sometimes, even the best audio needs some tweaking to eliminate the noise that may be inherent in a recording. This chapter outlines some noise reduction techniques, as well as some noise reduction plug-in choices that are available.

Getting good sound before requiring noise reduction

Hum, buzz, hiss, drone, swish, whisper and more are the sounds of noise on tape. It plagues amateurs and professionals alike in any number of situations, usually beyond the control of the videographer. Refrigerators, air conditioners, noise from air movement in the room, camera motors, zoom lenses, noisy cables, and electrical hum are just a few of the noise criminals that stalk an otherwise great video recording.

Wind, waterfalls, rivers, and traffic are all extremely difficult noises to remove, simply because the noise sources are constantly shifting the active frequencies, making the noise a constantly moving target. Trying to remove these elemental sounds from a recording is a significant challenge with even the best noise reduction application.

Any video editor with a modicum of desire to have good video uses noise reduction of one kind or another. Understanding and practicing proper audio techniques can go a long way to getting a good signal on tape, yet sometimes or even many times, it is simply beyond rational ability to control.

Expect the audio to be compromised no matter how great the effort might be. If these are constant elements found in your video shoots, consider using hypercardioid microphones, shotgun mics inside of a good wind reduction system, lavaliers close to the sound source, or tightly held stick mics just out of camera range near the subject's mouth or sound source.

Always face away from the wind rather than into the wind so that air is not blowing across the microphone's plates. This sort of noise is nearly impossible to remove or significantly reduce. Get talent to speak as loudly as possible in noisy environs. It will often add to the drama of a noisy area, and will provide viewers with the most important part of the information related to the video; the spoken word.

Viewers will typically forgive less than stellar performances in challenging scenes if they can clearly hear what is being said. The bottom line is that it's far better to work on the front end of a production to prevent noise from entering the recording than it is to take the attitude that "you'll fix it in post."

Removing noise can be pleasurable or painful. In the end, it is absolutely better to do whatever it takes to minimize noise before the video shoot, but these pointers should help with the effort to remove noise that couldn't be controlled.

What types of noise reduction are available

Noise reduction tools come in two flavors only; good or inexpensive. There is no middle ground. Tools from WAVES, Bias, Cedar, and Sony are all highly effective noise reduction tools but they aren't inexpensive by any means. Equalizers are quite inexpensive, even free, yet are not terribly effective in most situations.

There are many noise reduction tools out there from which to choose, at all price points.

I'm partial to the WAVES and BIAS tools on the Apple platform and partial to the Sony tools on the Windows platform. I've had all three products save the day in otherwise bleak situations. Without this intending to be a review of the different products out there, I find that on the Apple platform, BIAS' SoundSoap Pro is the absolute gem of the heap.

On the PC side, it's a tossup, depending on budget. While the WAVES tools overall are superior plugins compared to most, Sony's Noise Reduction 2.0 has saved easily a thousand recordings over the past couple of years. It's slightly easier than WAVES, but also doesn't have the application integration with other noise reduction-oriented tools that WAVES has. When it comes to speed, Sony's tool is the fastest of any tool I've ever worked with, hardware or software based.

What Is Noise?

Noise is a series of frequencies that are part of an undesirable sound. Using Fast Fourier Transformation (FFT), the most effective noise reduction tools allow selective removal of troublesome frequencies. Consider FFT as being an EQ with more than 1000 bands of control, and that will set you on the right track of understanding.

Finding and isolating the noise-related frequencies from the desired frequencies contained in dialog or a performance is where the challenge comes in. Controlling them is even more challenging. This is where the beauty of any number of noise reduction software packages come in. Choosing a package isn't that difficult. Knowing how to use it effectively, can be.

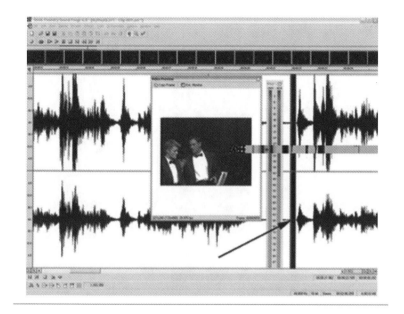

This image shows a video that contains a lot of room noise in the recording. The first step in the process of eliminating noise, is to find a section of the audio that contains only noise, no dialog, musical information, decay from a reverb in the room, or anything else except pure noise. In fact, it's a good idea on any video shoot to capture at least one minute of room ambience so that it might be used as a noise sample source in post-production. A "picture" or sample of this noise can then be taken, and used to compare with the noise in the production audio.

I've identified a section free of dialog, and have made a narrow selection of the noise. The selected area is actually fairly broad compared to the normal sample that should be taken. While the selection is only about .200 of a second, noise samples of less than .050 are typically desirable. Less information in the sample is generally better, but this particular file has a very well recorded dialog, so the signal to noise level is quite high.

Often, editors will attempt to remove all noise from a project with one process, and it is a serious mistake. Using very small time slices or selections, allows an editor to provide specific information to the noise reduction tool, with fewer and more specific frequencies contained in the noise sample. Using several noise samples, and multiple processes is one of the secrets to getting a good, clean file with significantly reduced noise.

The figure on the right is a zoomed in image displaying the selected area, it's relativity in volume or amplitude to the dialog contained in the audio file, and points out the noise we want to get rid of.

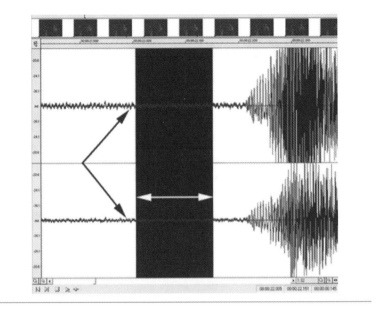

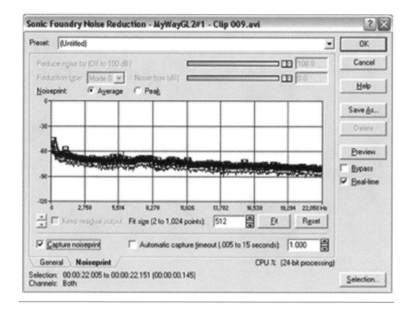

The figure on the left shows Sony's Noise Reduction 2.0's first dialog box. This has a check box to "Capture Noiseprint." A noiseprint is exactly as it's name implies, a picture, or "Print" of the noise contained in the selected area. By pressing the Preview button, an 'image' of the noise is created. The software will use this print as a means of comparing 'good' audio frequencies against the image, and selectively removing the 'bad' audio frequencies. The amount of removal is determined by the user with all of the software tools. A noiseprint profile may be saved by most of the noise reduction tools available, allowing the noiseprint to be applied to any files recorded in a particular environment. It's a good idea to store a noiseprint in the event that there is a lot of audio to be processed; some batch processing tools are capable of taking advantage of the noiseprint to remove noise in a large number of files in one processing path.

The figure on the right displays the audio file after the noise reduction software has been applied. Take note that the 'good' audio has not been visibly affected, and in fact, the ear can't hear any difference in the noise-cleaned file. All that is left is a solid, clean dialog. While it's in fact fairly rare to achieve complete removal of all noise without negatively affecting a dialog or music recording, if the signal to noise ratio is sufficient, and the dialog is clear and uncluttered with other noises, it's quite easy to get an extremely clean signal. Again, the secret is running multiple passes of whatever noise reduction tool you have access too, rather than attempting to do it all in one chunk.

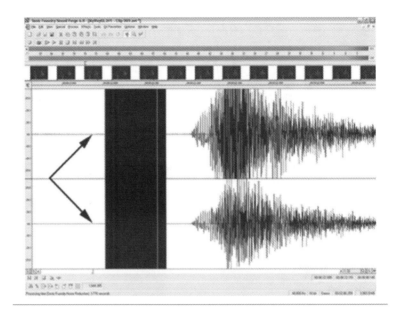

A few years back I was asked to do some forensic work on an audio file where a phone call had been recorded, but noise in the room caused the voice coming out of the ear piece of the telephone to be unintelligible. Since the noise source was fairly constant and the voice reasonably narrow in frequency response, I was able to remove the noise and provide a clean enough file for a stenographer to transcribe the audio to a text document.

To accomplish this however, it required somewhere in the neighborhood of 15 passes of the noise reduction tool, with extremely narrow selections of noise and careful tweaking of the amount of noise removed. Making matters worse was that I had to document each pass with exactly what was done to the file, and keep a comparison version of each pass for legal documentation. However, it worked very well, and in fact, I've now trained quite a few legal beagles in the use of noise reduction software.

But what if you don't have access to a good noise reduction software?

Remember that FFT is simply a monstrous algorithm that in the most simple terms is a large equalizer. Therefore, an EQ may be used to some effect, and if one is patient enough to stick with the numerous passes required to remove noise, then a marginal, and sometimes acceptable degree of noise reduction is possible. While not nearly as effective as a noise reduction application, it is indeed a poor man's method of achieving listenable results in many situations.

Graphic EQs rarely offer enough 'narrowing' of a frequency or band, and so a parametric EQ is really needed for this operation. Using a graphic equalizer without the ability to narrowly define a frequency range, will have an extremely negative impact on dialog or music that shares the same frequencies as the noise.

Sony's audio editing application, like many editing applications, offers a Spectrum Analysis tool, that provides a 'window' into the selected area seen here. Since we can see that the noise has a fairly high point relevant to the rest of the file at 7500Hz, it gives us an idea of where the equalization process should start at. Noise is often harmonic. Therefore, if you can find a tone in the harmonic, often times merely dividing the noise frequency in half, or doubling it provides a good clue to where to start the work of reducing noise.

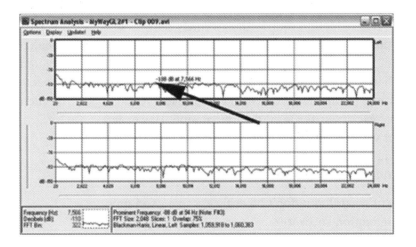

Once the frequency range is identified, the equalizer is opened, and the offending bands identified. At this point, set the paragraphic EQ to it's tightest "Q" setting, defining as few frequencies or bands as possible, allowing for the greatest control. This is going to take a while to accomplish, so be prepared to run this process several times. It's not going to reduce the noise very much with only a single pass.

In the image on page 157, we can see the noise level prior to using the EQ to reduce the noise in the selected area. It's currently peaking at approximately

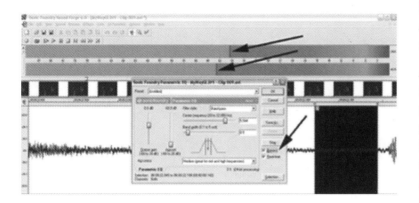

-56dB. The EQ is opened, but not enabled. Notice that the EQ is set for it's most narrow band width setting. Again, this is necessary to achieve noise reduction with an equalizer.

At this point, start working with the frequency identified by the spectrum analyzer, and preview the audio with the EQ enabled. Using the reduce/boost value found in the EQ, reduce the offending frequency all the way down. In this case, it's -40dB down. Slide the frequency around a bit, this might help you hear the effect the EQ is having on both the noise and the audio you wish to keep as natural and unprocessed.

Divide the offending frequency in half, and use that as your next starting point. In the case of the 7500Hz signal for instance, look at 3250Hz as the next point of attack. This won't be exact, but the math provides a good starting point. Again, run the process as described above, and repeat as necessary. Typically it will take at least 10 passes or more to achieve any real result using this type of noise reduction processing.

Notice how much noise has been reduced in this image, compared to the previous image. Using an EQ, the noise is somewhat reduced in comparison to where it was originally. It's absolutely not perfect, but better by comparison. Patience, attention to detail, and exceptionally narrow bands of frequency are all part of the noise reduction recipe. If a number of files are going to need noise cleanup, consider the costs of time versus results, as it might be that the purchase of noise reduction software will prove less expensive than the time required, not to mention that the results of the manual EQ processing are less than stellar compared to the much quicker and higher quality results of using a noise reduction application.

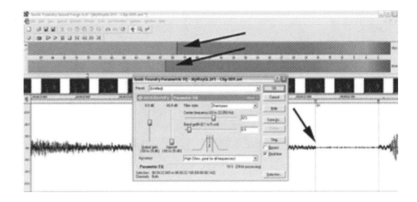

Particular care should be taken to set up exceptionally small noiseprints.

Practicing with noise reduction tools will also help train the ear to listen for noise, and assist in the production efforts to reduce noises in the shooting environment. Having a reasonably noise-free working environment is also important.

Computer fans, RAID fans, air conditioners without spillways, traffic sounds and other noise sources can all play a negative role in masking noise heard on your recording. While you should never mix with headphones, headphones are a good means of isolating and dealing with noise in your recordings. Check into noise suppression and room tuning products from companies like Auralex. For just a few dollars, you can make a significant impact on the ambient noise in your editing room while improving your overall listening environment.

Noise reduction, regardless of which brand you choose, is something that every video editor should own and know how to use well. All professional audio engineers have used these tools for many years. Using noise reduction and the tips I've talked about in this chapter can make the difference between good audio and great audio.

Chapter 12

Scouting the Location for Audio Problems

Recording audio, especially on location, is quite possibly one of the biggest challenges facing media creators. This chapter outlines some potential audio hazards and how to go about out trying to solve them.

Ambient Noise

Too much ambient noise is a common problem when shooting outside and is sometimes beyond a filmmaker's control. (you can't exactly make commercial airlines stop their flights just because you want to film). Sirens, cars whizzing by... in these situations you may have to simply wait until the excessive ambient sound dies down.

You may be able to take control of an excessive-noise situation depending on the circumstances. For example, if there is a group of kids nearby that are making too much noise, you may be able to diplomatically resolve the situation by asking them if it's all right to play somewhere else. Or you could use the age-old motivator: Money.

It goes without saying that microphone choice helps out here too, but the preferred method is to have it as quiet as you'd like without having to resort to repositioning mics.

Room Noise

A typical problem when shooting on location in a building is when a building's air conditioning and heating kicks in and turns off. A way to combat this problem is to turn the offending air conditioning or heating off. However, there are newer systems in buildings that can control an entire floor rather than a specific room. If you cannot get control of the system, block the offending vents with foam or other suitable material such as sound blankets.

Another source of building noise is lighting—typically, flourescent lighting. Ballasts in a flourescent fixture age, causing an annoying buzz that won't go away unless you turn the light off or remove the bulb.

Other sources of noise including the settling and creaking of a building, which, just like extraneous outside ambient noise, is beyond your control. The only thing to do in this situation is pay attention as you record.

Machinery Noise

Computers are notorious for their noise and are just as offensive when recording audio. Some systems are built to be very quiet nowadays but they're not as prevalent—at least not yet. For those systems that are noisy, you can place sound blankets around them, but be very careful as computers need adequate airflow to operate properly. Don't block a system's fan(s) if you can help it. Using sound blankets clipped to C stands might work quite well in this case.

Refrigerators and standalone air conditioners are a common source of noise as well. You can turn air conditioners off; a refrigerator can be unplugged or turned off but be sure to remind yourself that it's off. Closing doors or using sound blankets clipped to C stands will help out here as well.

Other sources of machinery noise are from computer monitors and TVs

Subject/Crew Noise

Tummies rumbling, heavy breathing, microphone rubbing/popping, clothing rubbing, shoe squeaking...these are just a few things that cause excessive noise.

Be sure that your subject and crew are still (more crew than anything; your subject may be required to have some action) and breathe slowly. Microphone rubbing and popping (especially on lapel-type mics) can be remedied by reminding the subject not to hit their chest and to remember where the mic is placed.

Corduroy, rayon and faux silk clothing are common fabrics that can send sound mixers into fits of rage. Have the subject wear clothing that's not as conductive.

Shoe squeaking and floors creaking can be a problem. Putting sawdust down can help cut down shoe squeaking on bare floors. Shoes can also be removed (especially if feet aren't to be shot) but can be hazardous due to all the heavy equipment around.

"Sticky mouth" is a common problem for talent. Be sure water is available to talent at all times. Voiceover talent swear by Granny Smith apples (they're the green type of apple) due to their ability to stabilize the saliva in one's mouth.

Gear Noise

Ground loops are a common problem with regard to equipment on location. The problem mainly occurs when using pro equipment with consumer-level equipment. Always use balanced XLR connections when possible.

Using wireless gear is always susceptible to noise. Digital wireless mics are getting better and better than their analog cousins. However, unless you don't have a choice, go with a wired setup for now.

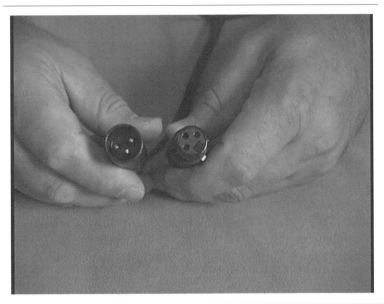

Video monitors, like other CRTs such as computer monitors and TVs, emit a carrier tone that can be heard and unintentionally captured. The carrier tone intensity varies from TV to TV. Either move the offending monitor or TV, or turn it off.

A high-quality mic mounting system, boom, zeppelin and windsock is essential, especially when recording outdoors.

Using these tips, you should be able to minimize or solve the problems you may encounter while recording out in the field.

Chapter 13

Simple, Practical Solutions for Difficult Edits

Say it with me: Digital audio editor. When it comes to difficult audio, a digital audio editor will be your best friend. This chapter discusses some great, practical ways of using such a tool to help you deal with difficult edits.

Editing on Consonants

Sometimes, consonants in a voice can seem too weak or not as pronounced as you would like them to be. An EQ can help in this case. By boosting certain frequencies, you can bring consonants back to life.

Due to varying circumstances in recordings, boosting frequencies is a matter of experimentation, but generally speaking, boost around 100-250Hz to add some punch, boost around 1-6kHz to add some presence.

When you make an edit, be sure that your edit begins and ends on a "zero crossing," or transient cut. This is the point at which the waveform crosses the baseline (at -Inf. or infinity). Ideally, the transient should have the same slope. This is so the audio doesn't "pop" when any edits are made.

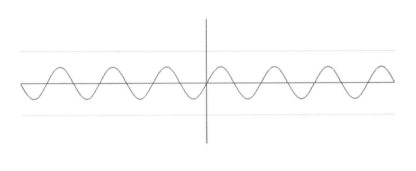

Alternative Editing Points

Muting

In certain cases, you may be tempted to use the mute command to silence ambient noise in a recording. Sometimes you may not want to do this because it won't sound natural in the scope of the whole recording. As an alternative, you can use a gentle fade envelope in your digital audio editor, or nonlinear editor.

Most digital audio editors and nonlinear editors let you use different fade curve types, such as a smooth or slow fade, in-between any two points for a smoother transition during the fade.

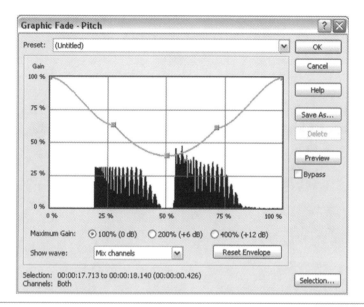

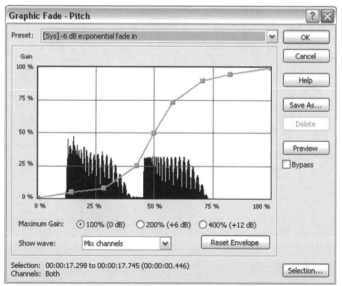

Simply activate the fade tool in your digital audio editor or nonlinear editor, then insert your points and drag as appropriate until it looks like a smile. Don't go too far in gain reduction; just enough so that the audio is not as noticeable but still there. You can probably dip the audio to a little below 25% of its original strength.

Do not delete the audio you want to get rid of, as that will affect the length of the audio track (effectively shrinking the length), which may be important especially if you need to line up the audio in a nonlinear editor. Instead, mute it.

Muting is OK to use on certain types of situations, like incoming audio for a video segment, and when you need to eliminate elements such as coughs and uhhh's. People tend to say, "uhh," all the time during an interview, which may be annoying. Since their mouth isn't doing much action, you can easily mute the "uhh" and nobody will know that it's gone because they never knew it was there.

Once you mute the problematic audio, the audio leading in may be a little unnatural sounding or abrupt. Use the fade tool provided by your DAW or NLE setup as noted before to create a gradual fade in so that the audio sounds more natural.

Noise Gates

Audio engineers tend to use noise gates a lot since they can also help problematic audio that has noise in-between dialog. However, the result can be somewhat harsh and artificial to the ear if not used correctly. You can see this by how abruptly the waveform is cut off rather than decaying naturally. Easy does it; a high threshold setting with a long decay can usually be beneficial but not overpowering.

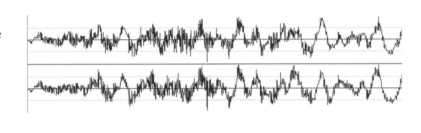

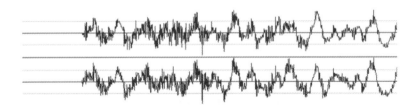

Chapter 14

Understanding Wireless Systems

Connecting Microphone and Camcorder

One of the best ways to assure bad audio is to use the microphone built into the camcorder. You're likely going to want to connect an external mic to the camcorder, and this segment will show you how it's done. Whether it's wired, or wireless, read on and discover the secrets of connecting sight and sound.

Cabled Microphones

There are effectively two types of cable runs that can be used to connect microphones and other equipment to each other; Balanced and Unbalanced. Both types of cables have their place, but for most video work, you're going to want to use balanced cables.

Line balancing originated with the telephone companies. This is how they sent audio over hundreds of miles without suffering signal loss and noise gain while using cheap wire. In your studio, you have dozens if not hundreds of potential noise sources, whether electromagnetic or transmission-based. Timecode generators, broadcast monitors, high powered amplifiers, DAT machines, power supplies, unshielded computer cases, basically anything that carries or creates a current is a potential noise source.

Moreover, cables are basically long antennas waiting to capture a signal.

When you connect a microphone to a mixer, preamp, or other source, you are completing a circuit. That circuit is constantly bombarded by electrical interference. Balanced cables allow the system to isolate itself from the electromagnetic or radio frequency (RF) interference.

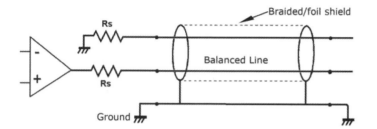

Two methods are employed to balance the line, depending on the equipment. Transformers may be used to balance the signal, and this is the method by which most higher cost equipment is balanced. Lines may be balanced electronically as well, and this is common in average to lower cost equipment.

Just because a cable has a low impedance connector or a TRS connector doesn't mean that it's balanced. There are different ways of wiring the cable, and while the line impedance might be balanced, the signal may not be. You want the signal and impedence to be balanced.

The simple way to expain this is that the impedance between pin 2 (in the 3-pin XLR or TRS) and ground is equivalent to the impedance between pin 3 and ground. But the signal is only present on pin 2. Pin 3 is the positive signal just like in the unbalanced coupling. Therefore the line is in balance, but not the signal. This is the most common method of balancing a line. The primary benefit of an unbalanced signal in the impedance-balanced coupling is that the amplitude of the signal will stay the same, regardless whether of the input connection is balanced or unbalanced, with or without an input transformer.

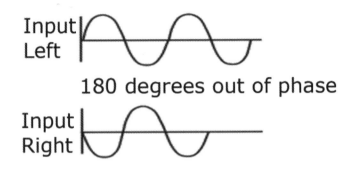

Essentially, with the phase inverted on one of the conductors, the difference in the voltage is the only thing that the recording equipment "hears." Noise is a constant, and so is ignored. This works much the same as a Difference Mask works in compositing; only what is different between two objects is allowed to pass through. Everything else is masked out.

Not all balanced connectors are the same. Here are two different balanced connectors.

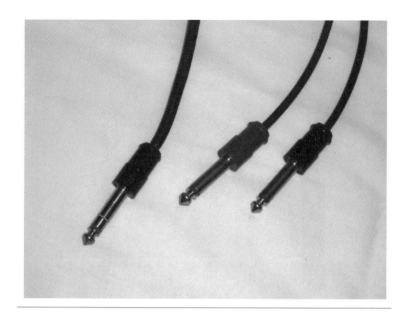

Be sure to never use a "Y" connector in a balanced connection. If you do, even though you'll hear audio on both channels/connectors, when the audio is mixed to mono, the two out-of-phase signals will cancel each other out. You'll have no audio at all.

When looking at a balanced cable, get a good cable and it will last a lifetime. Cable from manufacturers like Mogami or Canare is best, and their 4 pair cables (if cared for, will take nearly any abuse, but still coil neatly), is a little costly but a long-term investment. Strong and trustworthy cable is important, because the moment the integrity of the shield is compromised, the cable itself may be compromised. Shutting a door or equipment case on a cable may destroy it if the shield is broken or ruptured. You'll need to cut the cable to the point of damage and resolder the end. Of course, now you'll have two balanced cables in that situation.

One of the factors in choosing a good cable is knowing what kind of shield the cable has inside. Is it foil-wrapped, or is it braided? Foil marks a cheap cable, while braided shielding usually indicates a well-made cable. The better cables are also made with oxygen-free copper, or "OFC." Better cables are "SOW" or Sunlight, Oil, and Water resistant. If you're doing a lot of run'n'gun in a variety of areas, it's a good idea to consider this, especially if you're working in downtown streets where oil or water are expected.

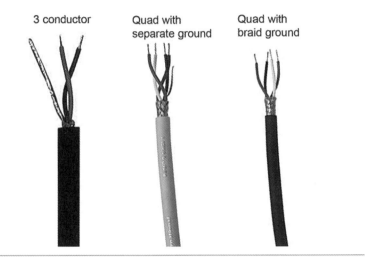

3 conductor Quad with separate ground Quad with braid ground

Connector quality is equally important. Good connectors from Switchcraft or Neutrik are long lasting, can be water resistant, and can withstand a reasonable amount of traffic. XLR connectors should always be used in field situations, as they are substantially stronger than their quarter inch counterpart.

The connector and wire coupling is important to how this all works. Any wire to the wrong pin or solder point, or if any strand of wire touches any of the other cable or pin points, there will be trouble.

There is no "standard", per se, how balanced cables are wired, but there is a generally accepted common method of how connections are made:

Pin 1-Ground	Tip-Hot
Pin 2-Hot	Ring-Cold
Pin 3-Cold	Sleeve-Ground

Sometimes in Europe, you'll run into older cables that are wired in reverse. Most mixers, digital audio workstations, and some NLE systems offer a phase invert switch. This reverses pins 2 and 3 on a standard connector. In the case of the DAW or NLE system, this invokes an inverted waveform. This may be necessary in some recordings. Of course, maintaining consistency in wiring is always the best thing you can do in order to keep phase or pin wiring from becoming a problem.

Generally, you want to connect all shields and ground everything. Use balanced cabling whenever possible, and on all cables longer than ten feet.

Unbalanced Cabling

Unbalanced cables are cables that don't offer protection from electromagnetic or RF interference. For very short runs, these cables are fine, but for anything longer than 10 feet or so, you'll likely run into interference problems. There are various grades of cable, and these will somewhat affect the distance that you'll be able to run cable without interference, but it's still a bad idea to try to extend the length if quality audio is your goal.

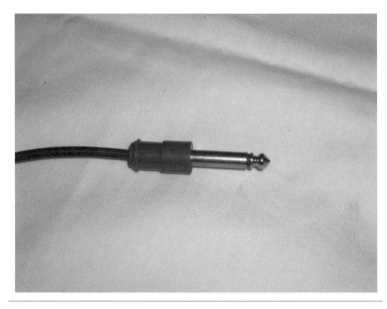

This type of connector is common in the video and audio world, and is often referred to as a "guitar cable, quarter-inch, Hi-Z, or phone cable."

Unbalanced cables can be connected in many different ways; RCA/phono plugs, 3.5mm (mini) plugs, 2.5mm (sub-mini plugs) are all common connections that are not balanced. While it's rare to find these cable types and these sorts of connectors in long lengths, with adapters, it's easy to make these cables longer. Just be aware of the potential challenges that you may face.

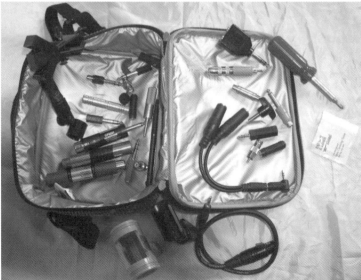

Connecting Balanced Cables to Unbalanced Inputs

All professional microphones are balanced output. Many pro-sumer camcorders do not have balanced inputs. Connecting a professional microphone to these sorts of cameras is fairly common, and shouldn't be a hassle. But it can be, if users aren't aware of how this is accomplished. Many users will run dozens of feet in balanced cable, only to terminate the cable with an unbalanced adapter. The moment this occurs, the entire cable run becomes unbalanced and interference or signal degradation is likely. There are a wide variety of manufacturers that build transformer balancing adapters for very little cost. The small Audio Technica adapters like this one can be found on various websites for as little as $15.00, and can be lifesavers.

Another option is to use a direct box, which is basically the same thing as the line transformer illustrated here. The direct box will take the balanced line as an input, and provide an unbalanced line output that can be directly connected to the camcorder.

A more costly, but certainly more elegant solution is to obtain a box from Beachtek or Studio One, but these do cost a bit more. However, they offer attenuation which may be needed in the event of a hot microphone, and most similar devices offer headphone outputs, line input/outputs, and some even, phantom power. These devices usually mount on the bottom of the camcorder, attaching to the tripod base. In turn, the audio converter has a tripod mount on the bottom so that the camcorder can be attached to the tripod just as the camera would have done.

These same devices may be employed in connecting a mixer to a camcorder. For example, if you are at an event that has a DJ and announcing system, you'll want to tie into the sound system whenever possible to capture audio from all microphones in the system. Either you'll need your own mixer with a splitter system or a "multi-box" or you'll need to connect to the room's sound system. Connecting to the room's sound system is much easier.

You'll want to connect from a sub mix output, or an auxiliary output if possible, so that whoever is controlling the mixing console can raise or lower their master volume without affecting what is being sent to the audio inputs on the camera.

The mixer output is likely going to be a line output. You'll need to use a padding device such as the one shown here.

Several companies manufacture these, varying in pad amounts of -5dB to as much as -50dB. These devices will take the output from the mixer and step it down to a level that the camcorder or convert device can accept. Some camcorders such as the Sony HVR-Z1U have line/mic switching built right in. In this event, you won't need to have a padding device.

Other Considerations When Working with Mic Cables

Aside from using quality cables and connectors, there are other methods of keeping your audio signal flow as clean as possible when connecting between microphones and camcorders or other recording devices.

For example, never run mic cables next to an electrical cable/extension cord. This can create problems in any event, and it's just good practice to keep low voltage cables away from high voltage cables.

Keep all audio equipment away from television monitors or other large transformer devices.

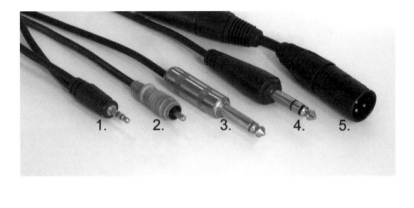

Use cables of appropriate length. If you have a 100' cable, but only need 5', you are leaving the remaining 95' coiled up. In the wrong area, this coil can actually act as a transformer coil, attracting or even generating noise if it's near an electromagnetic field.

Never coil/wrap cables around a table leg or center post just to keep it out of your way.

Carry a variety of adapters such as the ones you see here, in case of a situation arises where you'll need to connect to something uncommon to your normal production flow. I carry a wide assortment of these adapters in a padded bag that I purchased at Old Navy for about $5.00. These padded lunchboxes are great for carrying a variety of things.

Phantom Power-Ghosts in the Machine?

Phantom Power, also known as "plug in power," gets its name from being a power source that you can't really see. Condenser mics require power, and that power is sent from a variety of sources. Condenser microphones require a DC power source of 12-48 volts, and this power is usually sent down the microphone cable. For instance, some camcorders send power down the line, drawing voltage from the camcorder battery. Some condenser microphones eliminate the need to receive power via the cable and powering device by putting a battery compartment inside the microphone. If the mic has a built in battery compartment, the battery may usually be left in the microphone whether phantom power is available from a mixer or camcorder device or not. Most mixing consoles can provide phantom power. However, in the field, a mixer may simply be too much for a small production, and so other alternatives must be explored.

Aside from receiving power from a battery, camcorder, or mixing device, there are also stand-alone phantom power devices such as this Whirlwind box. It uses dual 9 volt batteries to power any microphone connected to it. If multiple mics need to be powered, there are devices that power up to 8 microphones per device.

Keep batteries fresh. As a battery loses voltage, the quality of the audio signal can be compromised. Don't let a production be compromised for want of a $3.00 battery. Use alkaline batteries, not rechargeables in your microphone or phantom device.

Finally, if your mix console or camcorder has switchable phantom power and you don't need to use phantom power, turn it off. Not only is it a power drain, but more importantly, if a mic cable isn't wired correctly, you could damage the device. If you have a mic cable that has been shorted, and you plug in a dynamic microphone, you could potentially damage the microphone. Or, if you are working with older microphones (very old) that have a center tap in the mic that's grounded to the mic body, it's also possible to damage the microphone, as the phantom power will likely blow the transformer. It's generally a safe assumption that if the microphone has a standard XLR connector, it's safe to use phantom power. The one exception to this rule is that ribbon mics can often be damaged by phantom power. Ribbon mics are rarely used in the video production world, so this should not be a common concern.

If you'd like to know more about the deep details of phantom power, the details are covered by DIN spec 45596, and there are many references. However, phantom power doesn't have any variables in terms of how it functions.

Wireless Systems

It's always best, when possible, to run cables to a camera.

Like the old saying says, "The shortest distance between two points is a straight line."

We've come a long way with radio transmission since 1899 when Marconi first sent a few signals across the English Channel. Thank heaven, because in this day and age, there are literally thousands of wireless transmissions taking place around us every moment of the day.

Don't run wireless systems simply because they are available. Introducing anything between a microphone and its destination is an added risk, regardless of the quality of the wireless system.

Sometimes cabling just isn't convenient, or long distances between microphone and camera may have obstacles that prevent sensible cable runs. Maybe the video shot won't work with a cable in it, or the action in the scene won't permit cables. Either way, wireless systems serve a valuable purpose these situations.

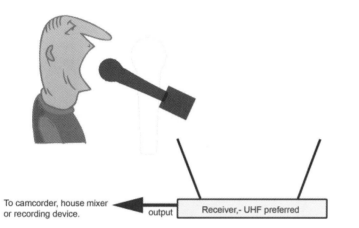

To camcorder, house mixer or recording device. ← output | Receiver,- UHF preferred

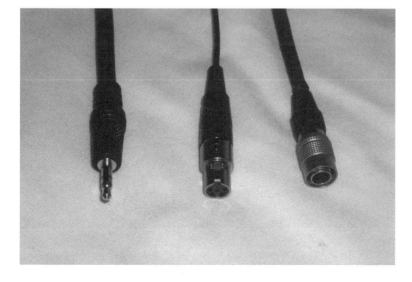

Wireless systems are available at virtually every price point. However, buying a wireless based on price alone, is a mistake you won't want to make.

There are essentially three components to the wireless system.

The transmitter

The receiver

The sound source (in our case, a microphone)

Nearly any microphone can be made wireless. There are essentially three connections that tie microphone and transmitter. Pictured here are the three major types of connectors.

3.5mm

Mini XLR

Hirose (Hee-roo-shee)

The 3.5mm is the least reliable and most potentially troublesome, while the mini-XLR is the most common. The Hirose connector is extremely sturdy, and can be counted on even in somewhat moist or humid situations. The Hirose is a little more difficult to solder, due to its construction, and its quite a bit more expensive. However, if the mic will be receiving a lot of hard use, the roadworthiness of the Hirose connector is proven and substantial.

There are two types of wireless systems that can be further broken down into smaller groups. Very High Frequency (VHF) systems, are the least expensive systems available, and are best suited for consumer use for home productions, close use for corporate video shoots, or other low budget productions. VHF systems don't sound any better or worse than their more expensive counterparts, but they are far more susceptible to interference.

Pictured here is the Audio Technica Pro88W wireless system. This is one of my preferred "low budget" systems. The reason that this is such a good system is that it offers no companding circuit.

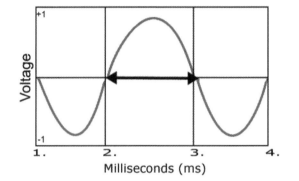

Voltage

+1

-1

1. 2. 3. 4.

Milliseconds (ms)

Virtually every wireless system in the market provides a compression/expansion system which compresses the audio signal before it's broadcast, and then at the receiver point, the signal is demodulated. The receiver then re-expands the audio signal. The reason this is done is to squeeze more audio information into a narrow bandwidth, and maintain a low noise floor. This is important, because direct radio transmissions can't achieve a signal to noise ratio of better than about 70dB. Most modern wireless systems can achieve a signal to noise ratio of up to 115dB, and very high end systems can push that value even further. However, in lower cost systems, companding also colors the sound and coupled with the lower quality microphones that often accompany the lower cost wireless systems, this can lead to severe coloration of the original sound. Still in the the VHF bandwidth, it's a good practice to be sure that you're working very close to the camcorder, or at the least very close to the receiver.

VHF systems are basically the same as FM radio. In fact, some of the least expensive systems actually allow or force you to use an FM receiver from a home stereo or something similar. VHF wireless systems also use the same frequency bands as the upper bands of analog television. VHF operates typically in the range of 169.5–212.8MHz (Megahertz) The biggest challenge with VHF is the long wavelength. Longer wavelengths mean that there is greater opportunity for interference. This is where UHF comes in.

Ultra High Frequency (UHF) systems are higher in frequency bandwidth, which means their wavelengths are shorter and therefore are less open to interference. UHF systems also carry a higher cost. However, if you're in a run-'n-gun production, or if the production team is moving from city to city, or even from one area to another area in the same city, UHF is the best option when wireless is required.

UHF systems also operate in the same frequency bandwidth as television, in about the same area as channels 38 through 70, or in the range of 650.1–806MHz (Megahertz). Up until recently, this has been great for users of wireless systems. However, with the advent digital television, you'll need to exercise greater diligence in checking your signal before a shoot. DTV doesn't allow as much free space in the bandwidth that analog television has offered us in the past. While the FCC has recently made allowances for this by opening up the 2.4 Gigahertz range for wireless mic systems, these are very expensive and not easily accessed. Further, wireless home telephones, microwaves and other devices also function in this frequency range.

DTV

Be sure that the UHF system has easily switchable channels. Both the receiver and the transmitter need to be able to change channels, and quickly. Audio Technica and other manufacturers provide a small screwdriver inside their transmitters, with knobs on the front of the receiver, allowing very fast channel changing. If you're doing a lot of wireless work and traveling from city to city, consider software that scans the area and provides a readout of what channels are available.

Always test your wireless gear prior to any recording, walking in a small grid area that the action will be taking place. Don't ever take wireless equipment for granted unless you've previously used it in the same location.

There are two variations of both UHF and VHF systems, known as "diversity" or "non-diversity." Diversity systems are the better of the two, as they offer some safeguards against dropouts that non diversity systems don't.

When a wireless transmitter sends out the radio signal, it bounces around the room or area in which it being used. If a reflection of the radio wave strikes the antenna of the wireless receiver at the same time as the original radio signal, it's likely to be an out of phase radio signal, and you'll experience a drop out. Diversity systems help safeguard against this issue by having two receiver circuits. The reason this works is that the chances of the same signal striking both antennas at the same time are very slim, and this helps protect the system from dropouts.

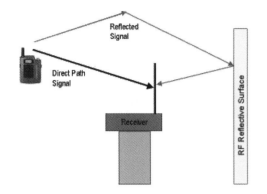

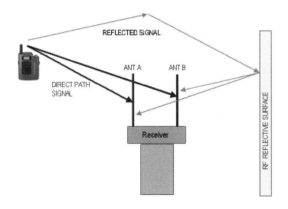

The diversity system antennas are not receiving simultaneously. The receiver switches when it detects a weak signal to noise ratio, and therefore receives a stronger signal on the opposite antenna. Diversity systems are constantly monitoring Signal to Noise Ratio. (SNR) Non-diversity systems have nothing to switch to, creating a potentially poor signal.

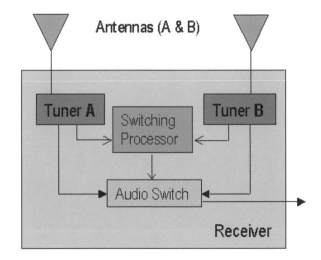

Antennas (A & B)

Tuner A | Switching Processor | Tuner B

Audio Switch

Receiver

There are two different methods in which the concept of diversity is employed. The first is Phase Diversity. This system uses two separate antennas but only one receiver. Lower costing systems use this type of technology. The better of the two options is the True Diversity system which uses two separate receivers with the two antennas. The two receivers look at the stronger of the two signals and makes a decision about which signal to accept. This costs more, but it's generally a good idea. If you're working in a big city, working in a metal building, restaurant, or shop with lots of motors, or computers, it's almost mandatory to have a true diversity system.

Finally, virtually all wireless systems have a Phase Locked Loop. In a PLL circuit, the radio signal is locked on a specific frequency and can also be used to generate, modulate and demodulate a signal and divide a frequency.

How to Use a Wireless System

Believe it or not, there are wrong ways, or rather less-than-optimal methods of using a wireless system. Any dense object regardless of what it's made of, can block the radio signal. Metal buildings, motors, lighting rigs, high voltage systems, transformers, even tin foil are all enemies of the wireless system. So is the human body.

If you're working with a wireless system where the receiver is on the camera as pictured here, then you don't need to worry much about the receiver side. However, if you're working with a rack mounted or cabinet mounted receiver, it's a good idea to consider an antenna extension, sometimes called a "booster." These stand-off devices sit away from the cabinet or rack where the wireless receiver is located. They will offer a much better better reception. Most wireless systems come equipped with quarter-wave antennas, while most antenna extender systems are half-wave systems. If you're running more than one wireless, some expander systems allow multiple receivers to be connected, splitting the signal to each receiver.

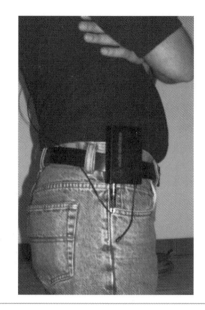

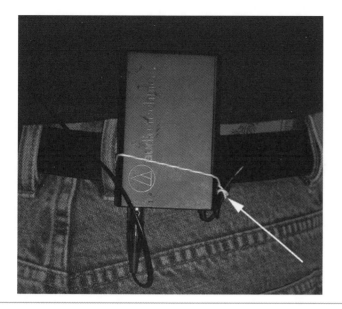

The location of the transmitter is where most people make mistakes.

First and foremost, never put the transmitter against bare skin on a performer or subject.

Don't put the wireless device behind the body if it can be avoided. The body is thick, and made mostly of water. Water is the enemy of radio waves and it's very possible to cause dropouts just by moving the wireless to the back of the body. Put the wireless transmitter on the hip, in a side pocket, or a jacket pocket when possible.

Let the transmitter antenna hang free. Don't fold, spindle, or mutilate the transmitter antenna. The more direct the line of sight between the transmitter and the receiver, the less the odds are of a dropout.

Don't ever allow the antenna and the mic cable to ever cross. While it's acceptable to loop the mic cable, the antenna should always be in a vertical position, either up or down. On film sets, it's common to see the sound team secure the antenna with a rubber band on the tip, and the other end of the rubber band secured straight down to an article of clothing. This keeps the antenna straight, but also allows the performer freedom of movement.

Body sweat can destroy the transmitter very quickly. Lectrosonics and some of the other very high end units offer seals that keep body sweat and other moisture sources out of the transmitter. If you don't have a high end system, no worries. There are a number of things you can do to help avoid sweat getting into the transmitter if you are limited on transmitter placement.

Use a dry, non-lubricated condom over the transmitter if you're in a wet area such as a swimming pool, humid climate, or if the subject simply has heavy perspiration. A standard condom will easily stretch over most transmitters.

Consider turning the transmitter upside down. Most transmitters will permit this. This will usually put the microphone connection, power switch, and antenna pointing toward the floor.

Spread antennas as far apart as possible.

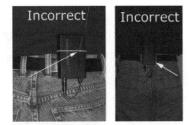

Keep the wireless antenna free, and prevent the body from being in between transmitter and receiver when possible.

Be sure that the transmitter is secure. A transmitter that flops around stands a good chance of dropouts, not to mention damage. A bit of gaffers tape is always good for holding the battery compartment on well-used wireless transmitters, and is always good to help hold down a loose wireless system. Avoid using duct tape (the silver stuff) on transmitters. Not only do some brands have metal in them, but they also usually leave behind a very sticky residue that gaffers tape won't.

Use flesh colored bandages to tape down a wire on a subject's body if the wire might be exposed to a video frame.

ACE bandages, or elastic bandages are good for securing wireless systems to a body in the thigh, ankle, or underarm area. If you'll be working with the same team/actors, or wardrobe, consider sewing permanent pockets into the wardrobe, or using industrial Velcro® to attach the transmitter to changeable wardrobe.

Always have fresh batteries on hand. 9 volt batteries are just over 9 volts when fresh, and will quickly deteriorate to 5-6 volts. This is problematic, because the wireless will have degraded audio signal below 8 volts or so. Newer systems are slightly more capable of lower voltages, but it's just common sense and good insurance to carry lots of extras. I buy them by the case at the local warehouse store. Expect about four to five hours of use from a 9 volt battery.

If you're planning on using rechargeable batteries, expect to change more often. Further, always check rechargeables before using them, and retire them after 6-8 months of heavy use. They'll gain a memory, even if they're lithium ion. Eventually they'll be good for about 5-10 minutes of use and no more. Personally, I don't trust rechargeables, mostly because I don't always have time to properly charge them.

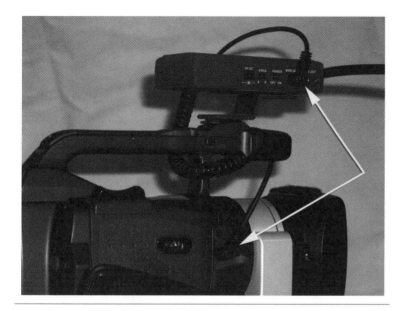

Carry a bit of soft foam and gaffers tape. Believe it or not, 9 volt batteries are as much as 1/16 different in length. This can be a problem in transmitters that are longer rather than shorter in the housing, and the battery can move around. Taping a tiny bit of foam to the bottom of the battery will prevent this from being a problem.

Understand that the wireless receiver doesn't need to be proximate to the camcorder or recording device. It's common practice on film sets and stages to put all the wireless receivers as close to the action as possible and run cables to the recording device. You can do this too. For example, on a wedding shoot, you could put the receiver very close to the bride and groom, still allowing them their freedom, but run cables to the camcorder or other recording device. This will also reduce the dropout and interference factor.

What About Handheld Wireless?

Handheld wireless is a slightly different concern than the bodypak or lavaliere transmitters. They either have the transmitter built directly into the microphone, or are plugs that can be attached to any microphone. Either works very well. The primary advantage of handheld is that the body is almost never directly between the receiver and the transmitter. The disadvantage is that the plug can make the mic a little longer and sometimes cumbersome, and it also requires the subject to hold it.

Multiple Wireless Transmitters

Of course you can have multiple wireless transmitters. You'll need to practice good frequency management once you get past eight units or so, but with some assistance, up to 60 channels can be operated simultaneously.

Always check the wireless systems one at a time, with all receivers turned on. If a transmitter is being picked up by more than one receiver, you'll see the other receiver(s) light up when you're testing the single unit. This is espe-

190MHz

195MHz

200Mhz

205Mhz

Add transmitter one and two, and subtract the frequency of transmitter three. Notice that the total is equal to the fourth mic's frequency? Therefore, you'll want to spread frequencies over the bandwidth with consideration for all of them combined. It's a good idea to maintain a spread of not less than .25MHz between operating frequencies.

Also, be sure to maintain distance to help avoid intermodulation, crosstalk, or other interference problems.

200MHz+195MHz-190MHz=**205MHz!**

cially critical when running more than two or three systems.

Proximity of one transmitter to another can also be a huge problem. If two actors are wearing wireless units and they are in a mock wrestle or hug, the two transmitters can be very, very close together. This can easily cause a problem. The two wireless transmitters, if on close frequencies, will intermodulate, and when the two transmitters are close, they can combine. This will cause RF feedback, somewhat like pointing a microphone directly into a speaker, so you'll want to be sure to check any transmitters that will be in close proximity. One analogy that we use on the road is that one frequency is blue, another is red. Mixed together, they make purple, which is a hue of both colors. Make sure the third wireless isn't in the "purple" range of colors. This is the safest way to run the devices.

What about using two transmitters on the same channel as one receiver?

Forget about it. Even if it were possible, the transmitters would be reaching the receiver at different times, either canceling each other out, or switching back and forth. Don't expect nor attempt to run two wireless transmitters to one receiver, unless you're interested in simply learning the effects of doing so. (you won't damage anything)

Did you know that you need a license to operate a wireless in the USA? Most people aren't aware of this little known requirement. A five year license carries a cost of $75.00 and takes about six to ten weeks to obtain. Yes indeed, the FCC requires a license. No one that sells wireless probably is even aware of this law, but it is there. Will anyone be punished for using a wireless system without a license? Likely not. Even as you read this, there are meetings taking place to determine if wireless networks in your home or office should require a license, so it's highly doubtful anyone will be knocking on your door for using a wireless system. However, if you are operating in the same frequency bandwidth as a licensed enterprise, you are required to change frequencies.

218-219 MHz SERVICE (PART 95)
(previously Interactive Video Data Service)

This radio service was converted to the Universal Licensing System (ULS). For information on ULS electronic filing, visit the Internet @ **http://wireless.fcc.gov/uls/**. The instructions that follow are for filing applications. Select the purpose of filing and follow the instructions below:

NEW or RENEWAL/MODIFICATION
- FCC 601 - FCC APPLICATION FOR WIRELESS TELECOMMUNICATIONS BUREAU RADIO SERVICE (FCC 601 – Editions prior to July 2005 are obsolete)
- FCC FORM 159 - FEE REMITTANCE ADVICE (FEBRUARY 2003 EDITION)
- Payment/Fee Type Code: PAIR - $555.00 FEE (per call sign)

MODIFICATION & NON-PROFIT (NONPROFIT filings must be accompanied with a current Determination Letter from the Internal Revenue Service documenting non-profit status under IRS Code Section 501 or a current certification as a nonprofit corporation or other nonprofit entity by state or other governmental authority)
- FCC 601 - FCC APPLICATION FOR WIRELESS TELECOMMUNICATIONS BUREAU RADIO SERVICE (FCC 601 – Editions prior to July 2005 are obsolete)
- FCC FORM 159 - FEE REMITTANCE ADVICE (FEBRUARY 2003 EDITION)
- Payment/Fee Type Code: PAIM - $55.00 FEE

ASSIGNMENTS OF AUTHORIZATION
- FCC 603 - FCC WIRELESS TELECOMMUNICATIONS BUREAU APPLICATION FOR ASSIGNMENTS OF AUTHORIZATION AND TRANSFERS OF CONTROL (FCC 603 – Editions prior to July 2005 are obsolete)
- FCC FORM 159 - FEE REMITTANCE ADVICE (FEBRUARY 2003 EDITION)
- Payment/Fee Type Code: PAIM - $55.00 FEE (per call sign)

TRANSFERS OF CONTROL
- FCC 603 - FCC WIRELESS TELECOMMUNICATIONS BUREAU APPLICATION FOR ASSIGNMENTS OF AUTHORIZATION AND TRANSFERS OF CONTROL (FCC 603 – Editions prior to July 2005 are obsolete)
- FCC FORM 159 - FEE REMITTANCE ADVICE (FEBRUARY 2003 EDITION)
- Payment/Fee Type Code: PATM - $55.00 FEE (per call sign)

SPECTRUM LEASING (Parties filing a De Facto Transfer Lease Application)
- FCC 603-T - FCC WIRELESS TELECOMMUNICATIONS BUREAU APPLICATION OR NOTIFICATION FOR SPECTRUM LEASING ARRANGEMENT (FCC 603-T – FEBRUARY 2004 EDITION)
- FCC FORM 159 - FEE REMITTANCE ADVICE (FEBRUARY 2003 EDITION)
- Payment/Fee Type Code: PATM - $55.00 FEE (per call sign/lease identifier)

Chapter 15

ACIDizing Digital Audio

Remember that one minute of ambient audio you recorded? What if you wanted to tweak the audio so that it loops properly when used as a general sound bed in Vegas, ACID Pro, SONAR, Soundtrack, or other applications that support ACIDized audio? This chapter goes into some detail on using Sound Forge and/or ACID Pro to do this. You can accomplish these same tasks with Soundtrack Pro as well; in this chapter, we're going to use Sound Forge for the purpose of brevity.

ACIDized Audio

ACIDized audio is simply audio that has an extra chunk of data embedded in it that a supporting application "reads" to determine what to do with that audio based upon the project's tempo and/or key (when applicable) and then stretching that audio (if necessary) to match the tempo and/or key.

For example, if you have an ACIDized loop that was ACIDized for 120 BPM (beats per minute) in the key of G, you can drop it into a project that's 130 BPM in a key of C and the application will automatically stretch the loop to match the project's tempo and key.

Because you might not deal with audio on a musically tonal level, you might not want to assign a key to an ACIDized loop. Thankfully, sounds that do not have a definite pitch can also be ACIDized by not assigning a root key to them.

It's important to know a few things before we begin. The most important thing to remember is that time and tempo are related. A sample of audio that's exactly two seconds long will fit perfectly within a tempo of 120 BPM (assuming we're talking common time here, where there are four beats to a measure and a quarter note gets a beat). There's a simple formula to use to help determine this:

$$240 / (\text{number of seconds}) = (\text{tempo})$$

Similarly, there is also a formula to determine the amount of time you need in a sample in order for it to fit perfectly within a given tempo:

$$240 / (tempo) = (number\ of\ seconds\ per\ measure)$$

You're probably wondering at this point, Why would I care about the time or tempo? Good question. There might be times where you'd like to use a particular ACIDized sample in an app that can recognize it. If you have ambient audio that rhythmically matches the music it may be paired with, wouldn't it be cool if it could stretch as appopriate if the tempo of the music changes as well?

Note that there's also a few different ACIDized forms of audio. Of particular concern to you would be the Loop and One-shot ACIDized track types. Loops can stretch key and tempo as appropriate, whereas One-shots are designed to play once in any given event and take a "what you hear is what you get" approach and do not change tempo or key even if the project does. As such, One-shots are great for vocal or sound effects "stabs" (hence their name).

Sound Forge

ACID Loop Creation Tools

Sound Forge has a set of tools for the express purpose of ACIDizing audio. By default, the toolbar for the ACID Loop Creation Tools itself is not visible. You can turn it on by going to View > Toolbars and then checking "ACID Loop Creation Tools."

Creating Loops

Creating Loops is a bit of a complicated affair. Not only should you tweak your sample so that it loops properly (see "Tweaking Your Samples" later on in this chapter), but you should also determine what is needed in order for the Loop to be read properly.

For example, if you have a minute or more of ambient audio, you could certainly turn that into a Loop, but be aware, as I've mentioned before, that time and tempo are related as far as the application that recognizes ACIDized audio is concerned. The sample must have the proper number of beats to be recognized in a particular tempo.

Sound Forge has an easy and quick way to find out just how many total beats there are in a file. Simply use the "Edit Tempo" button on the ACID Loop Creation Tools toolbar (make sure all or none of the file is selected).

Simply enter a tempo in the "tempo in beats per minute" field, and Sound Forge will tell you the selected length of beats the file has to be to fit within that tempo.

You can do this the hard way too if you don't have Sound Forge or similar editor.

Edit Tempo - Record Take 1.wav

Start:	00:00:06.857	hr:mn:sc.xxx	OK
End:	00:00:08.571		Cancel
Length:	00:00:01.714		Help
Input format:	Time		Play

Selection length in beats: 4.000

Tempo in beats per minute: 140.000

Number of beats in a measure: 4

☑ Play looped

As an example, let's say you have a sample that's forty seconds long. Let's say you want or need this sample to fit within a project tempo of 120 BPM. In order for that to happen, you must first determine how long a measure of audio will be. Use the formula to find how long a measure of audio will be:

There's a formula to use to determine the total number of beats (brace yourself):

So, taking our result from determining the number of seconds per measure, we complete our equation:

((40 seconds) / (2 seconds per measure)) x (4 beats per measure) = (80 beats)

I know this might make your head explode, but it's really not all that difficult. Try practicing with a few samples to see.

Edit Tempo - Record Take 1.wav

Start: `00:00:06.857` hr:mn:sc.xxx

End: `00:00:08.571`

Length: `00:00:01.714`

Input format: Time

Selection length in beats: `4.000`

Tempo in beats per minute: `140.000`

Number of beats in a measure: `4`

OK

Cancel

Help

Play

☑ Play looped

((total number of seconds of audio) / (number of seconds per measure)) x (number of beats per measure) = (total number of beats in sample)

You're now ready to take this final result and enter it via the Edit ACID Properties dialog window. You simply enter "80," as the number of beats, set the "root note for transposing" option to "don't transpose" and click OK. Then save your file.

When you bring your newly ACIDized Loop into an application that can recognize ACIDized audio, the application will deal with the audio appropriately. For example, when you bring the Loop into Vegas, Vegas will automatically timestretch the audio for you based upon the Vegas project's reference tempo (which is 120 BPM by default).

Setting the root note for transposing may depend on the source material; most ambient sounds, like traffic or a gurgling brook, don't have a definite pitch.

Be sure that, as with One-shots, you save your newly-ACIDized Loop with the "save metadata" option under the "Save As" dialog window.

In order for ACIDized audio to change tempo on a single track in Vegas, change the tempo of the project FIRST in Vegas, THEN add the same ACIDized audio to the track again on the timeline. It should then change tempo accordingly.

Creating One-shots

To create One-shots out of samples you have, modify and edit your audio as usual, making sure that the audio does not pop or click at the beginning or end of the file. (See, "Tweaking Your Samples," later in this chapter for tips.) Then click the "Edit ACID Properties" button on the ACID Loop Creation Tools toolbar.

The Edit ACID Properties dialog window opens. Click "One-Shot," then click, OK. Save your file. That's it! Your new file is ready to be used in an app that can recognize ACIDized audio.

ACID Pro

Creating Loops

When you create an ACIDized Loop in ACID Pro, you have a distinct advantage in that whatever Loops you create will automatically have the project's tempo and key (if applicable) applied to the created Loop.

To create a Loop in ACID Pro, you must bounce down using ACID's "render to new track" command. To do that:

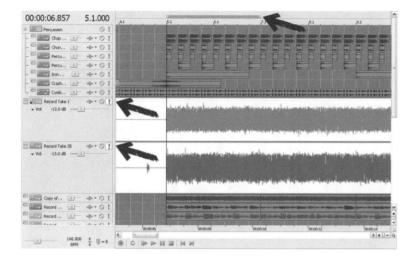

Isolate and solo the tracks you intend to make into a Loop. Place the Loop Region over only the area you'd like to keep.

Mix the track or tracks accordingly by getting them as loud as possible to unity (0.0 dBFS) without clipping.

Press Ctrl+M on your keyboard. The "Render to New Track" dialog window opens. Give your new track a name and check the "render loop region only" option. Click "Save". The newly rendered track is then added to your project.

You can then mute or delete the original tracks from your project. (Muting will not affect performance.) Paint or draw in your new track on the timeline to hear it.

If you're bouncing down audio that does not have a definite pitch, make sure you set the project's key to "None" before bouncing down. Otherwise, ACID will try key stretching the audio if project also changes key, making the audio sound unnatural.

By default, ACID creates Loops only if the sample being bounced down is between half a second to 30 seconds. You can change this by going to Options > Preferences on the menu bar and then clicking the Audio tab. Change the values in the "open files as loops if between" option. The maximum value is 300 seconds (or 5 minutes).

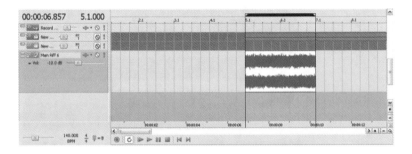

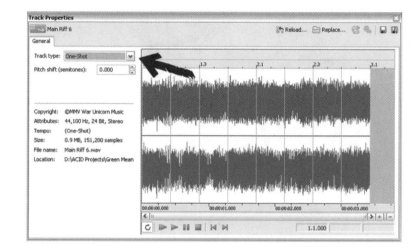

Creating One-shots

Creating One-shots is similar to creating Loops. However, by default, ACID creates a One-shot on the condition that the track being bounced down is less than half a second. That can be tough to do. However, you can easily go into the track's properties and change it to a One-shot. Just double-click the track's icon in the track list, then under the General tab, change "track type" to "One-shot."

If you want to permanently make the track a One-shot, be sure to click the "Save" icon in the track properties. Otherwise, ACID will assume that you just want to treat the track as a One-shot in the particular project you're working in.

Tweaking Your Samples

You obviously want to tweak your samples so that they sound their best, whether you intend to use them as One-shots or Loops.

For One-shots, make sure that the ends of the sample fade out properly at the beginning and end of the file so no sudden popping or glitching occurs when the One-shot plays back.

For Loops, you must make sure that the endpoints of the loops smoothly transition from end to beginning while they play back over and over. That's where Sound Forge's Loop Tuner comes in.

The Loop Tuner is only in the full version of Sound Forge, not Sound Forge Audio Studio.

Loop Tuner

Before we dig in with the Loop Tuner, we must first tell Sound Forge what kind of sample we want to work with. To do that, go to Special > Edit Sample on Sound Forge's menu bar.

Since we're want a loop that simply plays over and over, click "sustaining" for "sample type" and "infinite loop" immediately underneath. Click OK. You'll see that your sample now has sustaining loop markers. We need these markers for the Loop Tuner.

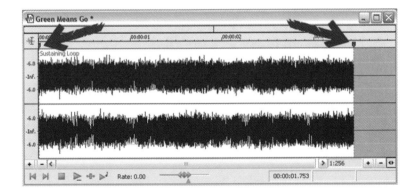

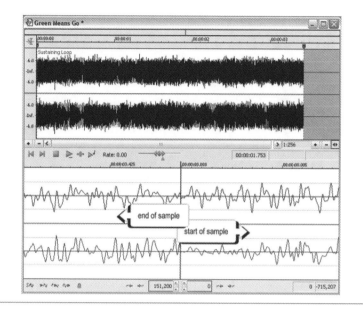

Now open the Loop Tuner by pressing Ctrl+Alt+L on your keyboard. You'll see that your sample's end position is on the left, while the sample's start position is on the right.

There are a few ways to ensure that the loop does not glitch as it repeats. One is to make sure that both endpoints end at a zero-crossing. A zero-crossing is the point at which a fluctuating signal crosses the baseline at –Inf.

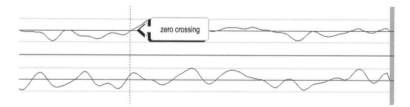

Another ideal tip to keep in mind is to match the endpoints' waveform slopes. If the end of the loop is sloping upward at a 45 degree angle, then the beginning of the loop should continue that 45 degree upward angle.

If you need to, you can use Sound Forge's Pencil Tool to adjust the slope at the endpoints of a loop if the audio is too glitchy.

The Loop Tuner has a couple tools that will come in handy to help fine-tune your endpoints. In each window for the endpoints, there is a "zero-crossing left" and "zero-crossing right" button. You can use these buttons to quickly find the nearest zero-crossing at the markers.

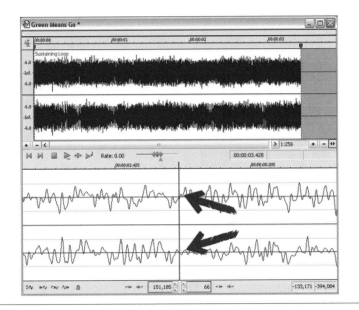

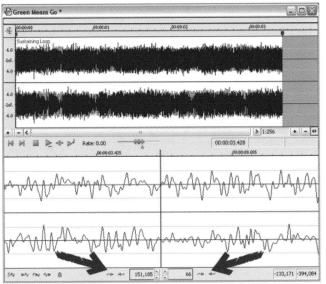

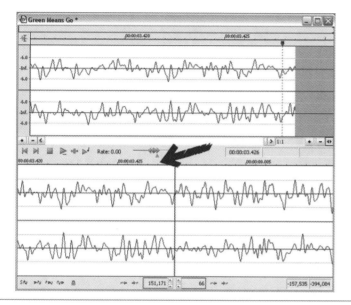

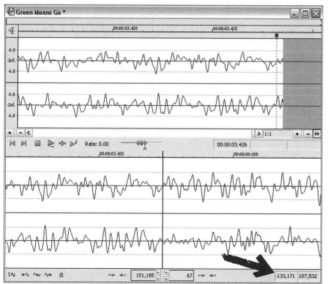

You can drag the ruler in the Loop Tuner to easily drag the end and beginning of the sample

In the bottom right corner of the Loop Tuner, there is an indicator telling you the amplitude for the end and the beginning of the loop. Ideally, these two readings should be close in value.

There are a few playback buttons in the Loop Tuner as well:

Play Pre-Loop – Lets you listen to just the data that's before the leftmost sustaining loop marker

Play Loop – Lets you listen to just the data in-between the two sustaining loop markers

Play Post-Loop – Lets you listen to just the data that's after the rightmost sustaining loop marker

The "Lock Loop Length" button lets you do just that; it will lock the length between the two sustaining loop markers so that you cannot make it shorter or longer.

There is also a "Play as Sample" button on the transport toolbar that functions similarly to the "Play Loop" button in the Loop Tuner.

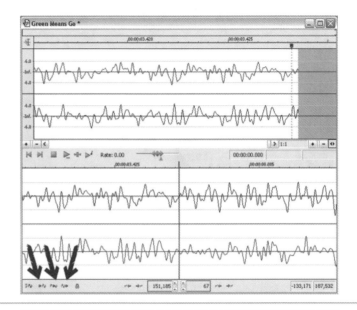

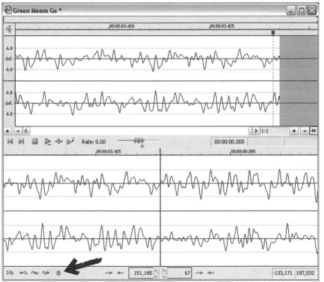

Once you do your tweaking in the Loop Tuner, you're more than likely left with extraneous data before and after the respective sustaining loop markers. You can delete the extraneous data, but remember that time affects tempo as mentioned before in this chapter. Shortening a sample increases its tempo. You can use the Tempo indicator on the ACID Loop Creation Tools toolbar to quickly gauge the tempo for your newly-edited sample.

Remember, this is based on a four beat sample using the length of the sample given. If there's too much of a drastic change in tempo, try Sound Forge's Time Stretch tool, located under Process > Time Stretch on the menu bar.

Tips and Tricks for Looped Audio

A common complaint you hear is that looped audio sounds too familiar as it loops over and over. There are a couple ways to overcome this.

One way is to use volume and pan envelopes to change the volume and panning of a particular loop so that it doesn't sound too uniform.

When using One-shots, a great way to make the audio sound irregular is to use several different One-shots painted out on the timeline. Coupled with the volume and panning envelopes tip, this can create a very convincing track that seems to be one long variable track rather than just an arranged set of limited samples.

This tip also works for Loops, but keep in mind Loops can be painted over and over again, unlike One-shots. To paint a single Loop or One-shot event in its entirety in ACID Pro, have the Paint Tool active and, while holding down Ctrl on your keyboard, click to place events on the timeline.

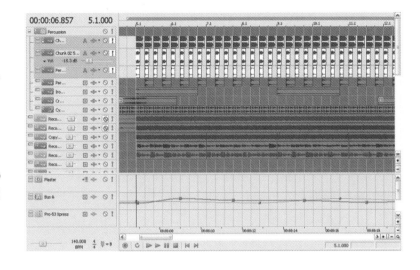

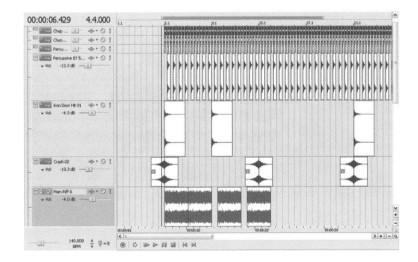

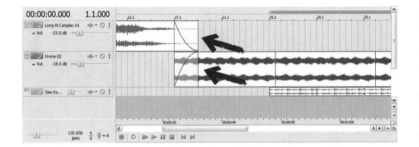

With Loops, consider erasing parts of an event irregularly (but not too much). For tracks whose Loop events that overlap on the timeline, select two events and press F on your keyboard. This will apply a quick fade between the two events for a smoother transition.

Use ACID Pro 5's Groove Tool to apply different "grooves" to Loops to make them sound different.

By creating your own Loops and One-shots from material you've recorded, you not only have created something original, but also something special by giving an extra layer of original flair to your projects. It is my hope that this chapter at least gave you a kick-start in that direction.

VASST is Video, Audio, Surround, and Streaming Training. Here at VASST we help you master your preferred topic faster than you ever expected with immediate, accessible and thorough information. We offer a variety of training materials for different learning styles.

Whether you are looking for a book, a DVD, or an on-site trainer, VASST can provide tips, techniques, and solutions for all your media needs.

VASST Training Tours: visit vasst.com for current tour dates. We offer seminars on Cameras, Lighting, Editing, Surround Sound, and other general media topics. Training on specific applications by companies such as Adobe, Sony, Ulead, Pinnacle, AVID, Boris, and Apple is also available.

Instant Sound Forge®
Jeffrey P. Fisher

Put this graphical cookbook of techniques to work in producing great audio with Sound Forge. Beginning with a review of the fundamental concepts, you get a complete guide to the audio production and post-production process with specific recipes for the most common challenges.

Softcover, 209 pp, ISBN 1-57820-244-2, $24.95

Instant Surround Sound
Jeffrey P. Fisher

Unravel the mysteries of multi-channel audio processing for musical and visual environments. This comprehensive resource teaches techniques for mixing, and encoding for surround sound. It is packed with tips and tricks that help the reader to avoid the most common (and uncommon) pitfalls.

$24.95, Softcover, 208 pp, ISBN 1-57820-246-9

Instant ACID®
John Rofrano and Iacobus

After reviewing the user interface, and the fundamentals of music theory and looping, you'll proceed to learn recording, adding effects, mixing and finally burning the project. Designed to be read as a complete tutorial, or as a quick reference guide, Instant ACID includes personal tips and workflow habits to help you become productive quickly.

Softcover, 240 pp, ISBN 1-57820-266-3, $24.95